Corporate Governance — How to Add Value to Your Company

A Practical Implementation Guide

Alex Knell

ELSEVIER

AMSTERDAM • BOSTON • HEIDELBERG • LONDON
NEW YORK • OXFORD • PARIS • SAN DIEGO
SAN FRANCISCO • SINGAPORE • SYDNEY • TOKYO

CIMA Publishing is an imprint of Elsevier

CIMA Publishing
An imprint of Elsevier
Linacre House, Jordan Hill, Oxford OX2 8DP
30 Corporate Drive, Burlington, MA 01803

First published 2006

British Library Cataloguing in Publication Data
A catalogue record for this book is available from the British Library

Library of Congress Cataloguing in Publication Data
A catalogue record for this book is available from the Library of Congress

ISBN 0 7506 6924 1
ISBN 978 0 7506 6924 5

For information on all CIMA Publishing Publications
visit our website at www.cimapublishing.com

Typeset by Cepha Imaging Pvt. Ltd, Bangalore, India
Printed and bound in Great Britain

Contents

Preface

Many entrepreneurs are focused so narrowly on the actual business of their company, they overlook processes and presentation. If the ultimate point in running a business is to realize wealth from a competitive advantage (and it should be), then the vehicle of the business itself must be polished and serviced.

It is not enough for those running the business to believe in it, its future and its value. It must be possible to show these qualities and pedigree to others – especially those who may already have, or wish to have, a stake in the business.

Corporate Governance (CG), through the Combined Code, provides a standard method for demonstrating this pedigree. It is designed for quoted PLCs. Applying CG principles voluntarily is a valeting service that will make the quality of your business shine and stand out from the rest.

An Overview of the Book

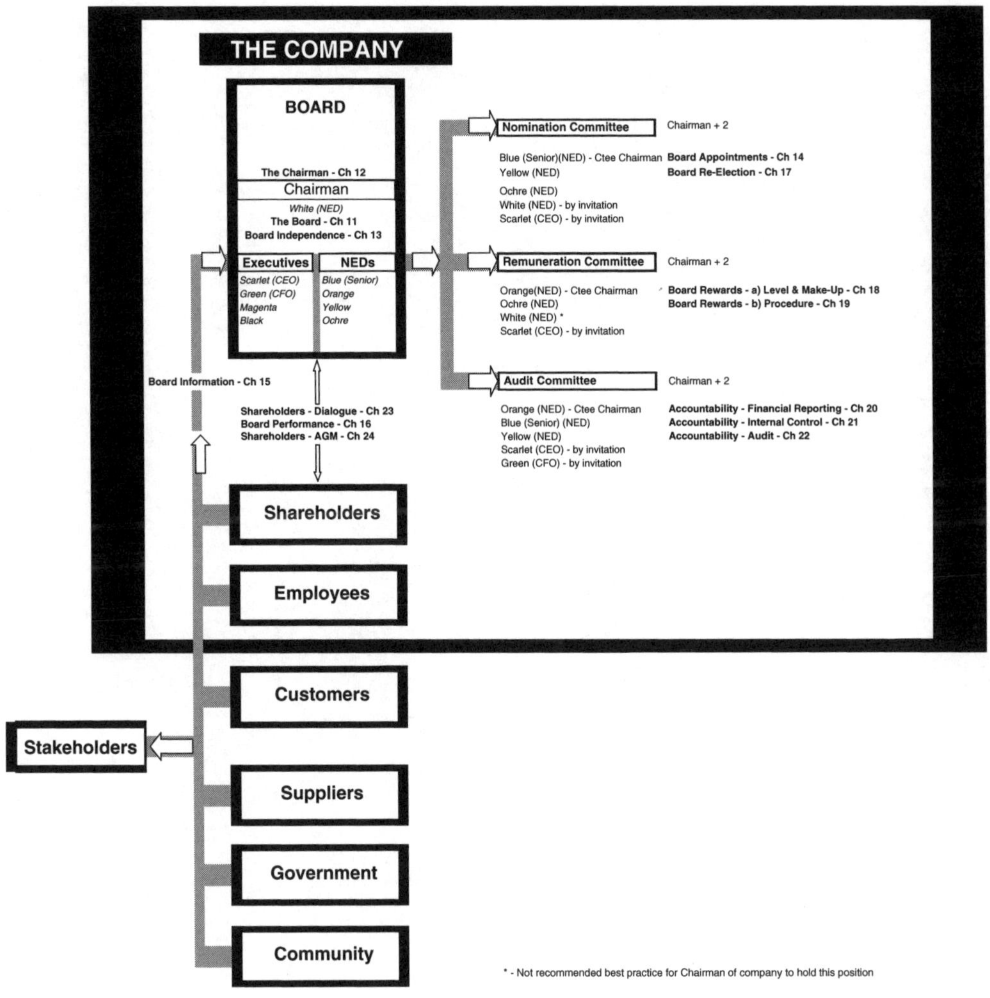

Figure 0.1

Acknowledgements

I acknowledge the exacting nature of my own company's Board – particularly the Non-Executive Directors. I had to rigorously examine the issues in this book and it was through this process that the commercial advantage of Corporate Governance (CG) became apparent.

However, without the unstinting support of Alison and all our children – Thomas, Melissa, Hannah and Richard – the time for this venture would never have even been a possibility. Also, the encouragement from Anne and my long-suffering parents made sure this book was completed.

Acknowledgements

Tell Me What I Need to Know about Corporate Governance (CG)...

Enhancing Value

Objective

The purpose of this book is to show you how to add value to your business.

It is primarily aimed at senior managers and directors of ambitious small and medium-sized enterprises (SMEs). Particularly, those with a view to selling all or part of their businesses – or an outright flotation in the medium term.

It is my contention that driving Corporate Governance (CG) into the fabric of your company has a similar impact on the value of your business, as adopting professional marketing techniques or quality standards. The potential buyer of your business perceives this value, and it is indeed real to your company.

So how much is your company worth? £2 million, £5 million, £20 million?
What if CG added a 10% premium to that price? Or more?
What if CG increased the pool of buyers at the asking price?
What if CG put your business at the top of someone's shopping list?
Then would it be worth implementing CG principles?

CG reduces the chance of Due Diligence failure. CG is now squarely on the radar of the Financial Reporting Council (FRC), who will review the compliance of listed companies from 2006.

In other words, the CG standards are here to stay and their demands are rising. Corporate Governance is not going out of fashion. The reasons for this are outlined cases like Enron and Worldcom, which will be dealt in Chapter 2.

What exactly is Corporate Governance (CG)?

Governance means to control and regulate; the exercise of influence to maintain good order and adherence to predetermined standards of behaviour.

Corporate Governance (CG) is the regulating influence applied to the affairs of a company to maintain good order and apply predetermined standards.

Put simply, CG is an ethical environment in which all business processes are undertaken. The predetermined standards are publicly known and are outlined in the Combined Code ('the Code'). Their application and regulation percolates throughout the business but must, naturally, emanate from the top – from the Board.

This is why CG concentrates on the Board so much – its Chairman, the objective balance of influence, delegation of authority, selection and re-election, remuneration, risk assessment, information provision, performance review, financial reporting and shareholder relations.

The expected standards are outlined in the Code. The 'serious' financial community is aware of what the Code demands since they deal with quoted plcs as a matter of course. Finding these standards applied in an unquoted company, *voluntarily* applied, is most impressive and unusual.

This is where the integrity factor makes a real difference to the marketability of a privately owned business. This is where voluntary compliance with CG adds value in the eyes of the buyer and enhances the realization of capital for the seller.

Consider the comments of Arthur Levitt, former Chairman of the Securities and Exchange Commission in the United States. In 2001 he said,

> 'If a country does not have a reputation for strong CG practice, capital will flow elsewhere.
> If investors are not confident with the level of disclosure, capital will flow elsewhere.
> If a country opts for lax accounting and reporting standards, capital will flow elsewhere.
> All enterprises in that country, regardless of how steadfast a particular company's practices, may suffer the consequences.
> Markets must now honour what they perhaps too often have failed to recognise.
> Markets exist by the grace of investors. And it is today's more empowered investors who will determine which companies and which markets will stand the test of time and endure the weight of greater competition'.

It serves us well to remember that no market has a divine right to investors' capital.

Arthur Levitt's reasoning holds no surprises for anyone. The argument for good CG has been present all along – it's as though we have needed a series of horrific disasters to make it a formal requirement. This is a similar situation to peoples' attitudes to drinking alcohol and driving a car. No one thinks it is a good idea to do it, but we need punishment laws anyway.

How to make things change

Using the unique ***ACCEPTS***™ method, the ***A***ccelerated ***C***ombined ***C***ode ***E***nabling ***P***lan and ***T***racking ***S***ystem, you can learn how to transform your business. This book explains, step by step, the processes required to achieve this. Some of the actions and changes are remarkably easy.

Based on the latest 2003 Combined Code, you can bring your business to a standard of CG which makes you stand out from a crowd. The way you visibly run your company will be in line with the highest standards, which has the added benefit of fewer changes to your processes after acquisition or flotation.

The ***ACCEPTS***™ method will guide you through the requirements of the Combined Code in an easy, no-nonsense manner. Using the method's unique scoring system, you will be able to track your company towards compliance.

Don't forget, as an SME you don't have to comply with any of this! It is only quoted plcs that must.

The book will help you prioritize your implementation areas of CG. By explaining what is being sought by the Code, it is also clear that how much has to be done. The explanations and checklists are there to help you. Be under no illusion that this is an overnight project. It is not. Nor is it a mere 'box-ticking' exercise. If you see your business being sold or floated in the next two years, or so, this is a good starting point to maximize your price.

The pay-off comes from your CG compliance because it is not compulsory. This is viewed as a voluntary baring of the soul, and is very well received.

Layout

This book is set out in two sections.

The first section addresses the basic theory underpinning CG. The purpose is to show the origin of the thinking that has been developed. An understanding of this will help you decide what compliance issues are immediately useful to your business, and which can wait. You can't do everything at once, so prioritizing is key.

The second section of the book explains the Code, section by section, indicating clearly what is being asked for. Each of the chapters in this section outlines the Code principles and has a 'translation' into plain English. It explains what needs to be done and provides a series of check-lists:

- things to be created or adopted;
- procedures to be created or implemented; and
- disclosures to be undertaken.

Many of these check-list items are shown in model form in the Appendices.

Finally, the unique ***ACCEPTS***™ method allows you to track your CG compliance progress over time. Each chapter in Section 2 has a CG compliance checklist, a copy of which is available as an Excel file from the author.

Results of compliance

Compliance means your company is 'punching above its weight' and is ready to advance to the next level.

Compliance shows your company is ambitious, forward thinking and progressive.

Compliance shows the Board to be dynamic.

Fulfilling all the recommendations of this book will not mean your business is prepared for flotation but in terms of CG you would be over 90% of the way there. Therefore, the Code demands will not be a millstone in the flotation process, as you will have much of this work completed.

The key thing to keep in mind is that CG compliance shows real confidence in the future and in the high growth prospects of your business. It is a frame of mind and an attitude that indicates real ambition and inspires those involved.

Remember, your business will be more attractive because it is visibly better managed and directed.

No CG Recognition – The Company You Keep

Proving a negative

If your company does not visibly observe CG principles, why should it make a difference?

The reason is that shareholders of quoted plcs have been burned so many times. Particularly and spectacularly in the last 20 years!
Fraud and greed scandals simply weaken investor confidence.
Less confidence means less active stock markets, which lead to lower or stagnating prices. Or no market.

The price of a share reflects all the information about that company in the market place. What if you can't trust that information, or you suspect there may be hidden facts? You won't buy that share or, if you do, you will not pay top price.

So, how do you tell investors that they have nothing to worry about and that you aren't hiding skeletons in your cupboard?

And don't be so naïve to think it is just investors who have an interest in your company. There are other *stakeholders* with an opinion of your business. What about your bank, your employees, your customers, your suppliers, etc.? This is discussed further in Chapter 7.

Recent history fuels anxiety

Just look at what happened after the 2001 Enron and WorldCom scandals. How could these global multi-billion dollar corporations, with clean audit certificates, suddenly collapse without any warning whatsoever?

The outcry from investors, employees and politicians reached fever pitch. Then suddenly, there was a procession of companies 'coming clean' about the inaccuracy of their reported numbers and stock market confidence nose-dived. Combined with 9/11 despair, most economies slumped.

The result of all this unpredictable/reckless/criminal behaviour has been an update of the Combined Code (the Code) in July 2003 in the United Kingdom, and the Sarbanes-Oxley Act 2002 (SOX) in the United States.

However, even in 2004, the mighty Royal Dutch Shell admitted to misreporting its reserves of oil. The share price plummeted in immediate reaction.

Curiously, the US had no CG regulation at all before SOX, leaving this role to the auditors. (Read on.)

In the UK, the intensity of CG regulation has grown significantly – but began with the Cadbury Report in 1992. Various UK scandals and bankruptcies have fuelled this, including BCCI, Robert Maxwell, Barings Bank, utility privatization scams, 'fat cat' salaries and bonuses, etc.

Let's have a brief look at two spectacular examples where CG observance may have prevented, or at least reduced the scale of collapse – Enron and WorldCom.

Example 1 – Enron

Enron grew from a minor power supply agent to a global energy broker in 10 years. It grew into a complex monolith, the structure of which few understood. Unfortunately, Enron lost its focus on the energy industry and became seduced by the 'results management' industry.

Driven by growth, Enron's investors had an insatiable appetite for more. Ultimately, profits determined the level of executive bonuses. Profits also determined the value of executives' share options so that a rising share price – due to higher company earnings – made cheap share options more attractive. But there's only so much margin and so much growth to be had! So when this growth curve became unsustainable, other solutions were required.

All along, huge stock options were offered to senior executives. The hidden cost of these was not expensed, while all of it was tax-deductible.

If a person is awarded a $10 share option and the market price of a share reaches $60, 'exercising' that option to buy a share costs $10, with an immediate sale value of $60 – an instant $50 profit. 100,000 options gives a personal $5 million profit, paid for by shareholders. Enron was famous for 'mega-grants' of options, producing mega-profits to the executives concerned.

The impact of this was to encourage senior executives to lie, cheat and manipulate earnings in any way they could to maximize the share price, and thus, the value of their options.

Between 1998 and 2000 the total salary, bonuses, exercised options and perks paid to Enron's CEO, Kenneth Lay, was $211 million. Enron President, Jeffrey Skilling, was rewarded to the tune of $130 million during that same period.

Enron also encouraged imaginative schemes that worked within the accounting rules, but only generated paper profits. Unfortunately, many of these schemes had no economic substance or basis in reality.

For example, Enron could create a partnership, then trade with it. To a reasonable person it would be obvious that, if Enron were the only customer in this partnership, any profit made by Enron would be a loss to the partnership, and vice versa.

When accounting for both Enron and the partnership, the net profit or loss would be zero. A zero-sum game.

Now, what if you could engineer a scheme where Enron made the profit, the partnership made an equivalent loss – but Enron didn't have to account for the partnership? Free profits and forget the losses!

In reality, if Enron kept its share of the partnership below 97%, then Enron did not have to account for the partnership losses at all. This was referred to as 'garaging losses'. The supporting borrowings were also 'garaged'.

Enron had over 4,000 of these partnerships – often with Enron staff as the partners – at the time of its collapse. Bonuses were paid to staff on the basis of these 'profits'. All borrowings surrounding these partnership ventures remained 'off balance sheet', so investors had no idea about the mountain of debt Enron had hidden from view, either.

These tactics were playing to a weakness in the financial reporting system and were wholly unethical. The fabulous sustained growth had no basis in reality and the senior executives are facing long prison sentences to reflect on this.

Unfortunately for the investors, the (then) prestigious auditors Arthur Andersen were complicit. Enron represented the largest audit at the

Houston office of Arthur Andersen. The audit fees were dwarfed by consulting fees.

It is thought that much of these fees had been paid for advice to devise or make workable the accounting engineering tricks mentioned above.

The world will never know the extent of this complicity as tons of papers were famously shredded by the auditors. Today, the act of auditors shredding documents carries up to 25 years in jail.

Ultimately, it was a Whistle-blower – an employee, not an auditor – who brought Enron down.

The Enron CG scandal was a major reason for the demise of Arthur Andersen's audit business. However, they were also the auditors for WorldCom.

Example 2 – WorldCom

WorldCom was, as the name suggests, a major player in the global communications industry. It had meteoric growth during its short life.

In this case too, WorldCom lost its focus on the communications industry and became seduced by the 'results management' industry.

Again, the investors' insatiable appetite for earnings growth made the company look elsewhere for it. Again, the growth curve became unsustainable and other solutions had to be found.

WorldCom's cheats were simple and completely at the opposite end of the ingenuity spectrum when compared to Enron.

Any junior auditor should have picked up these scams. Try these:

- You sign a 20-year line rental contract with a customer for $1 million per year. In the first year, how much rental income would you book? $1 million is the right answer. WorldCom booked $20 million. (Yes, all of it.)
- When you run a business you buy big items, like machines, and capitalize them. You then spread the cost over 5 or 10 years, or whatever the useful life of the machine is.

How about capitalizing all of the day-to-day running costs as well? That would make this year's results look good, deferring these running costs until future years. WorldCom did this on a massive scale.

Again, a huge deception. Again, a sudden corporate collapse.

Incidentally, remember who the auditors were? Arthur Andersen.

Solution – keeping businesses honest

In both Enron and WorldCom, the rot stemmed from the top. A regime of dishonesty was encouraged and few had the nerve to blow the whistle.

- The executives involved were totally driven by their personal reward structure.
- Boardrooms were stacked out with lavishly rewarded friends who would not create waves or ask difficult questions.
- The independent Non-Executive Directors (NEDs) were heavily rewarded and their independence was questionable.
- The watchdogs (auditors) were bribed with generous non-audit work, making their audit report somewhat fanciful.

Everywhere a conflict of interests! Let's look at each of the above again:

- Executives being driven by a personal reward structure is fine provided it is aligned with the prosperity of the company and, thus, the shareholders' wealth. Clearly, executives who create personal wealth from unexpensed costs, mis-reported financial statements or accounting gymnastics are creating nothing for the shareholders while heartily lining their own pockets.
- Filling the boardroom with well-rewarded nodding cronies gives a disproportionate amount of power to a small number of directors. These cronies are rarely present due to merit, and this places a disproportionate burden on the independent NEDs to maintain balance.
- Giving lavish rewards to the independent NEDs soon knocks the independence out of them! They are less inclined to ask difficult questions once their price is reached.

- Repeating this trick with the auditors by giving them consulting fees that dwarf the audit fee. Or even offer the audit partner a place on your board, just in case he was thinking of changing jobs. The audit certificate loses its gloss once you build in a few compromises.

A framework of recognized CG criteria, endorsed and implemented from the top of the company, is the only way to create the confidence that an ethical culture exists. This is not logically foolproof as criminals will always find a way to break the law.

But if you believe most people are decent and honest, CG *compliance* gives a company so many honesty boundaries to publicly cross that dishonesty is unlikely to persist unchallenged, unnoticed or unpublicized.

Therefore, publicly adopting CG compliance is great news for all the stakeholders who deal with your company. A fact that does not go unnoticed by a potential buyer of your business.

Why No CG?

We saw in the previous chapter how companies can behave when there is no ethical leadership. Bearing this in mind, there are 10 common reasons for not implementing formal CG compliance.

How many of them do you think are valid?

1. It's too complicated

   There are no complicated concepts involved at all (see *Chapter 4*).

2. It's too time consuming

   It is true that there is time involved in setting up the structures. However, many elements are one-off issues and you are probably doing some already, but are not disclosing the situation properly.

   The purpose of this book is to simplify the CG compliance process, and you will be guided at every stage. You can take it as quickly or as slowly as you like.

3. I want to keep control – I'm the Chairman (I don't need another one!)

   This can be a major issue for some companies, particularly of the smaller, family type. A company is only worth something if it can demonstrate revenue streams into the future. Keeping the gene-pool in the Board narrowed will not enhance the future success of the business. It is a well-known concern that the majority of family companies fail by the third generation. If your stakeholders have this kind of opinion, how can you benefit the future of your business by maintaining the status quo?

4. I've heard it's a waste of time

   Calling CG 'a waste of time' (whose time?) is a bit like patriotism – in the eighteenth century, Samuel Johnson referred to patriotism as 'the last refuge of the scoundrel'. A scoundrel will not vote for CG, as inevitably as a turkey will not vote for Christmas. Samuel Johnson also said,

   > *'Integrity without knowledge is weak and useless, and knowledge without integrity is dangerous and dreadful'.*

We have graphically seen the effects of 'knowledge without integrity' on the shareholders and employees of Enron and WorldCom.

5. I don't want to involve outsiders

   See 3. Which is more important – the long-term success of the business, or the privacy to fail quietly? Bringing non-executive experience to the Board is a breath of fresh air to strategic thinking. To use the analogy again, widening the gene-pool increases the probability of success.

   A group of like-minded people may well solve a problem. However, the number of different solutions (from which one is selected) will be narrower than if the problem were given to a more diverse group.

   The primary role of the Board is to encourage strategic thinking and develop future strategic plans. Involving NEDs is vital to widening the creativity of this process and adding credibility using the benefit of their experience.

6. I'll never find the right people to be NEDs

   A good NED should be a skilled, experienced business person. Good at *business*.

   If he or she is familiar with your industry and region, that's just great. The principles of success, profit and growth are what a NED should radiate at the selection interview. The idea is to lean on NEDs to benefit from their experience so that you don't have to re-invent the wheel.

7. I can't afford NEDs

   NEDs are not expensive. One of the central CG concepts concerning NEDs is their independence. This limits the earnings of NEDs since, otherwise, they would be dependent and no longer impartial.

   Being realistic, NEDs do not do this for the money. The pride of seeing another business thrive on the strength of their advice and guidance is a major incentive.

So beware – you need to choose NEDs who are right for you, but you also need to sell your company to the prospective NEDs!

8. Who will organize all this?

   A good 'Company Secretary' will really shine if given the responsibility of implementing these requirements. If your existing Company Secretary is a director in dual role (e.g. the Finance Director is also the Company Secretary), consider splitting the role or contracting a 'temp' agency to perform your implementation.

   These days, the job of a Company Secretary is complex – see *Chapter 6*. It is a significant compliance risk to leave this role to chance.

9. Nice idea, but where would I start?

   You already have. The purpose of this book is to show you how to address each CG area and measure your improvement towards substantial compliance.

10. Nice idea, but how will I keep this running?

    A good Company Secretary is the answer to this question too.

Basic Concepts

The basic concepts underlying 'Corporate Governance' are things our parents taught us as children. There is nothing surprising and there are no revelations. These concepts are discussed below and more practically applied in the next section.

Openness
A willingness to provide information.

Honesty
Telling the story truthfully and without spin.

Transparency
Visibility and clarity of processes and procedures.

A code of ethics

Based on guidelines for moral behaviour, a code of ethics can be developed to encourage appropriate behaviour. So, guided by a sense of right and wrong (the underlying moral values), a code of ethical conduct can be developed to which people may be expected to abide.

People must make judgements about whether an action is right or wrong under an ethical code. Some people will therefore regard such a code as guidelines to the way they behave. Others will regard it as an obstacle to be circumvented.

Conflicts of interests in business

Conflicts of interests can lead to ethical or moral dilemmas.

They often occur in business and should be resolved by honest and trustworthy negotiation.

In the absence of ethical conduct, he who wields the most power gets his own way – whether good or bad for the business. This can lead to breaking rules, corruption and personal interests winning the day.

The New York Stock Exchange (NYSE) set out a number of areas an ethical code should deal with:

- the avoidance of conflicts of interests
- opportunities for personal gain
- confidentiality
- fair dealings with stakeholders

- appropriate use and protection of corporate assets
- legal compliance
- the encouragement of Whistle-blowing.

As is seen later, the Combined Code ('the Code') combats conflicts of interests by adding independence and objectivity to the Board, largely through the use of Non-Executive Directors (NEDs).

Applied Concepts

Having discussed Openness, Honesty, Transparency and Ethical Conduct, we can now examine how they are applied in the business environment. These are the core issues upon which all CG is based – every rule.

Independence

This is the state that exists when there is no conflict of interests. People are able to act objectively. Examples where independence *no longer applies* illustrate the point best:

- auditors developing significant fee-earning non-audit work – they may be reluctant to risk losing the *non-audit work* if they uncover a major problem in the audit and may be compromised.
- auditors becoming highly dependent on a single client – they may be reluctant to risk losing the *client* if they uncover a major problem in the audit and may be compromised.
- NEDs receiving significant remuneration, options or bonuses – they may be reluctant to dissuade the Board from engaging in questionable business practices or creative financial reporting if a major reward is pending and may be compromised.
- NEDs remain with the company for many years – they may be reluctant to argue with members of the Board who have become friends and may be compromised.
- Chairman and CEO are the same person – the temptation is to wield power as a CEO and 'rubber stamp' the actions through the Board, emasculating the Board which may be compromised.

As you can see, the demonstration of independence is a basic necessity in the credibility of any CG initiative.

Responsibility

With authority comes the responsibility to be accountable to those on whose behalf they act. For example, the Board is given the authority by the company to act on the company's behalf. The Board is, therefore, responsible to the company for its actions.

Accountability

This is the requirement of those in authority, and exercising responsibility, to justify and explain their actions – to those on whose behalf they act. For example, directors are accountable to their shareholders.

Fairness

Impartiality and lack of bias together with reasonable and consistent behaviour.

This is particularly relevant, for example, with respect to minority shareholders and their interests.

Reputation

A company's reputation is built up over a period of time and is the sum of all knowledge of those who interact with it. Reputation is sometimes viewed as the 'intangible share price'.

It is a reflection of the company's ethics in its dealings with customers, suppliers and staff, together with its interaction with the communities in which it operates.

And a company's reputation can be lost overnight.

Loss of reputation destroyed Arthur Andersen's audit business completely and globally. Their name used to be prestigious and command respect. Now it is in the gutter with Enron.

6 Director's Duties – A Reminder

A company is run by its directors on behalf of the shareholders. In smaller companies directors and shareholders may be the same people. However, the duties of a director are clear, and should be distinguished from those duties of an executive. The duties of an executive encompass the day-to-day running of the business.

So what are a director's duties?

Directors are agents of their company and have duties to the company itself. To be clear, these duties are not owed to its shareholders or employees. Directors are *accountable* to the shareholders, which is not the same thing. The concept is similar to having a duty to be loyal to your country, while having obligations to your community or family.

Statutory duties

Surprisingly, directors have very few statutory duties. The only requirements under the Companies Acts (1985, 1989) are:

- keep minutes of meetings; and
- submit company reports and accounts to the Registrar of Companies.

Fiduciary duties

These are more onerous and are aimed at making the director act in the best interests of the company, without profiting personally or secretly. This relates to agency and trust rules, and it stems from the fact that the directors control the company's assets without being the owners. The shareholders own the assets through the company, and it is irrelevant if the directors are also shareholders. They must always remember which hat they are wearing. Therefore, a director can only obtain a personal benefit from a company if the shareholders permit it. Avoidance of conflicts of interests is the key to preventing a breach of this duty.

Duties of skill and care

These duties are difficult to define and are based on tests of reasonableness. The standards applied are based on how the person would have acted if the assets had belonged to them personally, compared to how they did act with the company's assets.

Thus, in matters of scientific research an accountant would be expected to have lower expertise than a scientist. And a scientist would be expected to have lower expertise in finance than an accountant.

These things are considered in making an assessment of reasonable skill. A director should not act negligently, otherwise he will be personally liable for that action and any loss caused by a negligent action.

The most dangerous area here is trading while insolvent. If the company is going bust and, as a director, you knew (or should reasonably have known) then you may become personally liable for the company's debts.

Other and emerging legal obligations

Directors should be aware that the buck also stops with them in a number of other areas. A good Company Secretary should keep the Board compliant (see below), but some of the sundry legislation a director has responsibilities under, include:

- *Data Protection Act 1998*
- *Company Directors Disqualification Act 1986*
- *Contracts (Rights of Third Parties) Act 1999*
- *Employment Act 2002*
- *Employment Rights Act 1996*
- *Employment Relations Act 1999*
- *Health & Safety at Work Act 1974*
- *Management of Health & Safety at Work Regulations 1999*
- *Reporting of Injuries, Diseases and Dangerous Occurrences Regulations (RIDDOR) 1986*
- *Fixed Term Employees (Prevention of Less Favourable Treatment) Regulations 2002*
- *Part Time Employees (Prevention of Less Favourable Treatment) Regulations 2000*

- *Transfer of Undertakings (Protection of Employment) Regulations (TUPE) 1981*
- *Working Time Regulations 1998*

This list is not exhaustive.

Executive and Non-Executive Directors (NEDs)

The law makes no distinction between executive and Non-Executive Directors. The Board is collectively responsible for all of its decisions. You may conclude from this chapter that NEDs are precariously placed. On the one hand, their rewards must be modest to maintain their independence. On the other hand they are equally responsible for the Board's decisions (and equally liable). Your conclusion is correct! This is why NEDs are at the heart of good CG.

Company Secretary

There has been such an enormous increase in compliance legislation that a 'part-time' or 'convenient' (e.g. wife/husband) Company Secretary is no longer a safe option. Someone within the business should be familiar with compliance issues emanating from the Companies Acts, employment law, insurance law, copyright law, pensions, environmental regulations, etc. (see above).

Ignorance of the law has never been an excuse. The Company Secretary is the obvious choice to maintain a company's compliance – or outsource the role through an agency.

7

Who are the Other Stakeholders?

There are more people interested in the success of your business than just the shareholders. Other groups also have some influence on the success, or otherwise, of your business. The opinions of these groups do matter and can be positively enhanced by the implementation of CG.

Company workforce

Of all the people involved in your business, this group must have confidence in the way the business is managed. They see the business from the inside and can judge for themselves if the business is ethically oriented. If this group does not feel comfortable with the way their company is managed, success cannot happen.

Conversely, deliberate reassurance through CG is a strong encouragement that things are done properly and the Board is open to scrutiny.

Banks and lenders

Banks and other lenders have no way of knowing the internal workings of your business. They have contact with senior executives and a relationship of trust can develop. CG implementation is a highly reassuring initiative, leading to greater voluntary disclosure and openness. It is a declaration of ethical behaviour that is well received.

Customers

CG provides a significant insight into the organization and running of your business. You show that you have taken on these virtuous concepts, endorsing your credibility as a serious partner to the customers' business.

Suppliers

How liable is your business to 'sudden-death' between audited annual accounts, in the same way as Enron and WorldCom were? How much credit should be risked by your suppliers?

To what degree does their confidence in your business suffer because you do not demonstrate the reassurance of CG?

Government

HM Revenue and Customs are very happy to see an ethical boost to your business processes. There is an implicit security to their receipt of taxes and for honest dealing.

Time will tell if this reduces the number of visits received from them!

Local community

A business that espouses CG declares a social conscience. Local communities are happy to have socially responsible companies operating within them. These companies provide employment and, for example, minimize their polluted outputs, contribute towards the provision of local sports facilities, etc.

Other

There are other groups that have an interest in the business, such as competitors, economists, politicians and anyone else upon whose world your business impinges. What you do also makes an impression on each of them.

Summary

It is worth considering who each of these stakeholder groups are, and evaluating their influence on your business. Then consider the impact of CG implementation on each group.

Will they appreciate that you are 'punching above your weight' in compliance terms? That your business is forward thinking, progressive and ambitious? That the Board is dynamic and ethical?

Will they appreciate that you have great confidence in the future and in the high growth prospects of your business?

Will they appreciate that your business is visibly better managed and directed?

The answer should be 'yes'!

The Key Areas Addressed by CG

It is an interesting fact that good quality systems implemented to comply with ISO 900X permeate all aspects of a business. All the way to senior management level. There only exclusion is the Board. There are no quality standards for the Board.

CG provides these standards. CG identifies the areas of weakness, as illustrated and highlighted by a history of various frauds, sudden corporate failures and sundry abuses.

The principles and concepts identified in Chapters 4 and 5 are now brought into action. They are applied to the five key dimensions of the Board's power and behaviour. These are:

- Decision-making powers
- Risk-taking
- Directors' remuneration
- Financial reporting and auditing; and
- Communications between directors and shareholders

Each will be outlined in turn to explain its relevance. The areas of weakness will also be discussed, each of which are addressed by the Code itself.

Decision-making powers

When the Board makes a decision, all directors, executive or NED, are equally responsible for that decision. So the Board should be effective and directors should be forthcoming with their opinions.

To prevent autocracies (one-man-bands), a number of experienced and independent NEDs should be on the Board to promote objective and informed debate. Ideally, the number of NEDs should balance the executives in equal numbers. The appointment of an independent NED Chairman rounds off this objectivity.

It is vital that a list of issues is developed that *must* be referred to the Board. This means no individual Executive Director can make decisions on these issues alone. This can only work in practice if the Board also meets regularly!

The independence of the NEDs should be further implemented in the areas of pay (Remuneration Committee), appointment (Nomination Committee) and reporting (Audit Committee – see below).

The policy of how Directors Remuneration is awarded should be agreed with shareholders and implemented by the NEDs.

There is a popular movement to increase the powers of shareholders, thereby having more influence over the Board. However, even the most ardent activist will admit that shareholders do not make full use of their powers – such as for the re-election of directors – so how will giving them more help? Self-regulation must begin with a balanced Board.

Risk-taking

In any business, a balance is struck between risk and return. Every transaction presents a possibility of loss to a lesser or greater degree. Hence, in high risk businesses, high returns should be expected and low returns from low risk businesses.

Investors should be aware of the prevailing risk climate in which a business operates and will expect a commensurate return. CG alerts the Board to increased risk, thus making shareholders feel confident that the Board is aware of the risks the company is facing.

Take-overs are a good example where a Board directly faces the risk/return dilemma, which manifests itself as 'how much should we pay for this business?'

It has been a common event that the acquiring company may pay too much, especially if more than one serious buyer is involved. This overpayment may give the Board higher status and a larger business, but it is gained at the expense of the depletion of shareholder wealth, and increased financial risk.

Directors' remuneration

Scandals of huge salaries and bonuses have been rife. They make popular headlines and increase the overall level of public cynicism.

Institutional shareholders, who hold the bulk of shares on the London and New York stock markets, invest your pension fund and insurance premiums. They do not object to high levels of remuneration being paid providing they track company performance and mirror shareholder success. The main complaint is the reward for failure.

There is little that will infuriate a shareholder more than seeing their Board of Directors helping themselves to performance bonuses at the same time as profits fall, the share price drops and/or dividends are cut.

The only thing that comes close is when a Director resigns (or is resigned) and takes a big terminal payment to ease the pain.

Rubbing salt in the wounds, some termination terms have included share options. Shareholders will, rightly, be bewildered by the reasoning for giving a share in the company's future success (the share option) as a reward for failing the company.

The only objective way to pay Executive Directors fairly is to take it out of their hands and prevent them from paying themselves. The NEDs, through the Remuneration Committee, set policy and criteria for determining the levels of pay, benefits, options and bonuses.

As we know, NEDs should be paid modest salaries, without share options or bonuses, and are not the subject of controversy.

A serious difficulty with the remuneration of Executive Directors is phasing. The Remuneration Committee may, for example, be criticized for rewarding success on a long-term strategy, which in the short-term, sees profits fall. Thus, bonuses may be paid to the Executive Directors as profits fall (public information), yet success in the agreed strategy said this would happen (not public information). Is the Remuneration Committee wrong?

The Board deals in long-term issues, so the annual reporting cycle may be inadequate to reflect the reasons for bonuses on some occasions.

So, even Remuneration Committees may be criticized. But, having one should prevent the public display of greed and cynical self-interest that Executive Directors have shown their stakeholders in the past.

Financial reporting and auditing

In Chapter 2, we saw the examples of Enron and WorldCom. The published Annual Reports and Accounts of these two global organizations were misleading as they approached their respective failures. They were depicted as vibrant, prosperous and talented businesses.

Their published success knew no bounds. Everyone wanted to invest in them, including their own employees with their pension funds (now mostly lost).

So how could these monolithic organizations fail so suddenly when they had been reporting continuous success?

There are only two explanations, either or both of which must be true.

First, the published financial statements are plainly false and do not reflect sensible or honest accounting practices. This means the accounts are 'window dressed' (deliberately misleading) or just plain wrong.

Second, the effectiveness of the auditors comes into question.

It is the job of management, not the auditors, to detect fraud. There is a strong movement to make this the case.

Missing something is bad enough, but being corrupted and turning a 'blind eye' to questionable practices is another thing. There has been a great deal of discussion on the level of non-audit consultancy work that a company's auditors should be allowed to do. The answer seems to be 'very little'.

It is worth reiterating the words of Arthur Levitt here, the former Chairman of the Securities and Exchange Commission in the United States. In 2001, he said,

> 'If a country does not have a reputation for strong CG practice, capital will flow elsewhere. If investors are not confident with the level of disclosure, capital will flow elsewhere. If a country opts for lax accounting and reporting standards, capital will flow elsewhere. All enterprises in that country, regardless of how steadfast a particular company's practices, may suffer the consequences. Markets must now honour what they perhaps too often have failed to recognise. Markets exist by the grace of investors. And it is today's more empowered investors who will determine which companies and which markets will stand the test of time and endure the weight of greater competition. It serves us well to remember that no market has a divine right to investors' capital'.

Remember that these large-scale economic difficulties percolate down through large- and medium-sized businesses to affect the environment of the small businesses, too.

SMEs can differentiate themselves by observing the CG recommendations and adding further credibility to their Financial Statements. Credibility adds premium.

Communications between directors and shareholders

For SMEs, this is not often a major issue.

Frequently, the number of shareholders is very small. Sometimes the only reason for a significant number of shareholders is that the company has a share incentive scheme and, as the workforce has grown, so has the shareholder base.

The Board should do what it can, by way of providing information, to make shareholders feel genuinely part of something. Making the most of the Annual General Meeting as an opportunity to meet with shareholders is strongly recommended.

There is a great deal in the Code about relationships with institutional shareholders. Unquoted companies rarely have dealings with this type of shareholder, except in the case of venture capital companies – with whom the company's directors will invariably be closely involved.

The *ACCEPTS*™ Method

What is the *ACCEPTS*™ Method?

The *ACCEPTS*™ Method is a logical, step-by-step approach to CG implementation. It uses the Combined Code ('the Code') as its basis.

The rules have been grouped together logically into sections. Each section of the Code is introduced in plain English, to illustrate the thinking behind it. Each broad Code requirement is then broken down into single, manageable components that are easy to understand and follow. A suggestion is given for compliance to each component, and a reference authority is given wherever possible. Following the analysis of each section, there are three checklists:

- Things to be created or adopted;
- Procedures to be created or implemented; and
- Disclosures to be undertaken.

Many of these items are demonstrated in the Appendices to save you time. Finally, there is a coherent method for tracking the progress of your implementation using the unique scoring system.

Scoring Chart – *ACCEPTS*™ Method Instructions

For each section of the Combined Code, there is a specially constructed checklist. Each provision is also broken down into discrete components.

Thus, if a provision has five components, failing one component means you fail the entire provision. This does not help you to monitor your progress very easily.

Under the *ACCEPTS*™ *System*, you will not only be monitoring your compliance with each provision, but will also be monitoring your compliance with each of the individual components.

So, when we have a provision with five components, failing one component means you still fail the provision, but score 4 out of 5 at component level. It is this component breakdown that makes the *ACCEPTS*™ *System* unique.

The instructions for the score charts at the end of each chapter in Section 2 are as follows:

1. Go to the end of the chapter and find the Score Chart.

2. Familiarize yourself with the Principle in this section.

3. Insert a date in the first available (slanted) column to the right of the Principle.
4. Read each Code component. If you are compliant, mark the small box with a '1' (directly below the date box), otherwise leave it as a '0'.
   You may wish to make notes in the space provided beside *Steps Taken*. This can be what you did to gain compliance, or what you intend to do.
   Refer back to the *Components in this Section* tables in the chapter if you are unclear about any of the Code requirements.
5. When you have completed this process for all components, add up the number of '1's and enter the total at the bottom in the *Results* section in the *Components* line.
6. Now inspect how many complete provisions you have complied with, and enter a total at the bottom in the *Results* section on the *Provisions* line.
7. You may now calculate your percentage compliance for both Components and Provisions.
8. Transcribe these totals from the *Results* section of this page to the *Grand Score Chart* on page 197, under the appropriate date.
9. On the *Grand Score Chart* you should compile all the results from all sections of the code to develop the overall picture.
10. You may now calculate your overall percentage compliance for both Components and Provisions.
11. On each of your chosen dates, you can monitor your overall compliance progress.

It is best if you review all sections in one exercise to determine your overall status and progress.

Excel® spreadsheet

An integrated Excel® spreadsheet model of all the individual score sheets and the *Grand Score Chart* (on page 197) is enclosed with this book.

Basic Steps

Positioning principle

There is no getting away from the need to 'beef up' your Board with experienced and independent Non-Executive Directors (NEDs). This isn't as horrifying as it sounds and can provide your company with a great deal of wisdom at an economical price.

Remember that it is very flattering to be asked to be a NED, consequently they don't cost a lot and NEDs must respect confidentiality.

A NED should be prepared to give your company 1–2 days each month.

To ease the implementation process, having a competent, ICSA-qualified Company Secretary is also desirable.

In plain English?

A number of CG compliance issues depend on NEDs.

However, you do not have to wait until they are in place to begin this compliance process.

They can be slotted into their roles as they become available. A good Company Secretary will make all this happen faster and easier.

What needs to be done?

Today, there is positive encouragement for Executive Directors of quoted plcs to hold a NED position elsewhere.

You need to start this recruitment process at the earliest opportunity.

Get your Company Secretary on a crash-course in Corporate Governance.

Ensure you look at people with a good track record and, if possible, those that have some financial fluency.

Also, ensure that any of the potential candidates *can* really give your business the time you feel that you need.

Checklists

Where to find NEDs:

IOD
Local Chamber of Trade
Head-hunters
Advertising

See:

Appendix 5: Guidance on the Role of Non-Executive Director;
Appendix 6: Sample Letter of Non-Executive Director Appointment; and
Appendix 15: CG Role of the Company Secretary.

Detailed Implementation ...

The Board

What is the principle?

Every company should be headed by an effective Board, which is collectively responsible for the success of the company.

Supporting principles

The Board's role is to provide entrepreneurial leadership of the company within a framework of prudent and effective controls which enables risk to be assessed and managed.

The Board should set the company's strategic aims, ensure that the necessary financial and human resources are in place for the company to meet its objectives and review management performance.

The Board should set the company's values and standards and ensure that its obligations to its shareholders and others are understood and met.

All directors must take decisions objectively in the interests of the company.

As part of their role as members of a unitary board, Non-Executive Directors (NEDs) should:

- constructively challenge and help develop proposals on strategy;
- scrutinize the performance of management in meeting agreed goals and objectives and monitor the reporting of performance;
- satisfy themselves on the integrity of financial information and that financial controls and systems of risk management are robust and defensible; and
- determine appropriate levels of remuneration of Executive Directors and have a prime role in appointing, and where necessary removing, Executive Directors, and in succession planning.

In plain English?

All members of the Board should have a say, not just one or two individuals. All members of the Board are equally responsible for all decisions.

The Board should collectively:

- provide entrepreneurial leadership;
- set strategy;

- control the level of risk exposure of the business;
- set the tone of the ethical environment.

The Board should collectively understand:

- the market place of the business;
- the needs of the stakeholders of the business;
- the personal responsibility of each director, executive or NED, to act in the company's best interests.

In addition, NEDs should:

- challenge management on its achievement of objectives and goals;
- review and evaluate monitoring and reporting systems;
- satisfy themselves with the integrity of the financial information produced;
- be comfortable with the effectiveness of risk management processes;
- be responsible for selecting, appointing and setting remuneration levels for Executive Directors; and
- be responsible for succession planning of Board and other senior positions.

What needs to be done?

The Board should meet on a regular basis. Four, six or 12 times each year is typical. There should be specific matters the Board keeps to itself. This means that the Board is *fully* involved in these matters – not just one or two Executive Directors making decisions alone. The ICSA recommend a checklist of items that should be reserved to the Board alone. This list should be tailored to include the most relevant items to your business. (See Appendix 2 – Matters Reserved for the Board).

The Board should set strategy by being fully familiar with the company's market place. It should devise plans to profitably delight the market place. Detailed functional supporting strategies, such as those for sales, operations and finance, should be brought to the Board by Executive Directors for approval.

Risk should always be on the same agenda as strategy. It is nonsensical to discuss long-term plans without involving the risk of success or failure, potential loss or gain.

Adherence to strategy and the level of risk should be monitored closely.

While it should be a concern of all directors, NEDs should be particularly comfortable with the standard, timeliness and integrity of financial information. NEDs should also be comfortable that risk levels are monitored closely.

NEDs should be appointed to the Board and be made responsible for recruiting and deciding the remuneration package of Executive Directors. There are a number of (new) disclosures to be made in the Annual Report. It is recommended that your company invest in a Directors & Officers (D & O) Insurance policy.

Components in this section:

Code Provisions	*Reference: Appendix*	*Example/Suggestion for Compliance*
A.1.1 The Board should meet sufficiently regularly to discharge its duties effectively.		The Board meets every month. Plan a rolling 15–12 month schedule. This is where a 15 month schedule is set, then allowed to run down to 12 months. It is then brought up to 15 months again.
There should be a formal schedule of matters specifically reserved for its decision.	Appendix 2: Matters Reserved for the Board	This should be created and approved by the Board and is a *crucial* document.
The Annual Report should include a statement of how the Board operates, including a high-level statement of which types of decisions are to be taken by the Board and which are to be delegated to management.	Appendix 1: Annual Report – CG Disclosures	A statement should be made in the Annual Report regarding Board operation. A full description of all committees, their policy, membership and frequency of meeting should be disclosed.

Continued

Code Provisions	*Reference: Appendix*	*Example/Suggestion for Compliance*
A.1.2 The Annual Report should identify the Chairman, the deputy Chairman (where there is one), the Chief Executive, the senior independent director and the Chairman and members of the Nomination, Audit and Remuneration Committees.	Appendix 1: Annual Report – CG Disclosures	Against each director's name, his or her executive role should be identified (CEO, CFO, etc). Similarly, the NED Chairman should be identified as well as the independent NEDs (if applicable).
It should also set out the number of meetings of the Board and those committees and individual attendance by directors.		A 'roll call' of directors. Easy to log and disclose.
A.1.3 The Chairman should hold meetings with the Non-Executive Directors without the executives present.		Arrange meeting. This is an opportunity to discuss the behaviour of the Board as a whole.
Led by the senior independent director, the Non-Executive Directors should meet without the Chairman present at least annually to appraise the Chairman's performance (as described in A.6.1) and on such other occasions as are deemed appropriate.		Arrange meeting. This is creating a performance review opportunity.
A.1.4 Where directors have concerns which cannot be resolved about the running of the company or a proposed action, they should ensure that their concerns are recorded in the Board minutes.		Careful minuting of Board meetings is essential. Where there is dissension, this should be clearly minuted. This has the effect of excluding a director from agreement to a particular collective Board decision.
On resignation, a Non-Executive Director		In all likelihood, this would probably happen, anyway.

Continued

Code Provisions	Reference: Appendix	Example/Suggestion for Compliance
A.1.4 (contd.) should provide a written statement to the Chairman, for circulation to the Board, if they have any such concerns.		Have the Board create the rule and minute it. Ensure the NEDs are aware of the rule.
A.1.5 The company should arrange appropriate insurance cover in respect of legal action against its directors.		The Code recommends that the Board insures its actions with a Directors & Officers (D & O) insurance policy. Most insurance brokers will arrange this.

Summary checklists

Things to be created or adopted

- A schedule of Board meetings for the next 15 months.
- A list of matters reserved for the Board.
- Minutes of Board Meetings and Board Committees to be maintained to a high standard.
- If not already in place, a Directors & Officers (D & O) insurance policy should be implemented.

Procedures to be created or implemented

- The Chairman should hold meetings without the Executive Directors being present to discuss any issues they see fit to discuss. (i.e. NEDs only).
- NEDs should meet without the Chairman to discuss the Chairman's performance at least once a year.
- Any director's unresolved concerns should be recorded in Board minutes.
- Any NED resigning with concerns should put those concerns in writing and the Chairman should circulate them to the Board.

Disclosures to be undertaken

- Annual Report statement of how the Board operates and functions, together with the purpose and policies of all committees.
- All Board members to be identified.
- All Committee positions to be identified.
- Disclose attendance by each director and frequency of Committee meetings.

See:

Appendix 1: Annual Report – CG Disclosures; and
Appendix 2: Matters Reserved for the Board.

Score Chart

Figure 11.1 on the following page is a chart for this section of the Code.

Please refer to *Scoring Chart – ACCEPTS™ Method Instructions* (on page 53).

Following the above instructions, complete this chart first, then transcribe your results to the *Grand Score Chart* on page 197.

Excel® spreadsheet

An integrated Excel® spreadsheet model of all the individual score sheets and the *Grand Score Chart* (on page 197) is enclosed with this book.

A	DIRECTORS	Chapter 11

A.1	The Board

Principle:

Every company should be headed by an effective Board, which is collectively responsible for the success of the company.

Code Provision			Date							Appendix	
A.1.1	The Board should meet sufficiently regularly to discharge its duties effectively.	Compliance	1	-	-	-	-	-	-		1 = "Yes" 0 = "No"
		Steps Taken								2	
	There should be a formal schedule of matters specifically reserved for its decision.	Compliance	1	-	-	-	-	-	-		1 = "Yes" 0 = "No"
		Steps Taken								1	
	The Annual Report should include a statement of how the Board operates, including a high level statement of which types of decisions are to be taken by the Board and which are to be delegated to management.	Compliance	1	-	-	-	-	-	-		1 = "Yes" 0 = "No"
		Steps Taken								1	

Code Provision											
A.1.2	The Annual Report should identify the chairman, the deputy chairman (where there is one), the chief executive, the senior independent director and the chairmen and members of the nomination, audit and Remuneration Committees.	Compliance	1	-	-	-	-	-	-		1 = "Yes" 0 = "No"
		Steps Taken								1	
	It should also set out the number of meetings of the Board and those committees and individual attendance by directors.	Compliance	1	-	-	-	-	-	-		1 = "Yes" 0 = "No"
		Steps Taken								1	

Figure 11.1

Code Provision		Compliance	1	-	-	-	-	-	-		1 = "Yes" 0 = "No"
A.1.3	The chairman should hold meetings with the non-executive directors without the executives present.	Steps Taken									
		Compliance	1	-	-	-	-	-	-		1 = "Yes" 0 = "No"
	Led by the senior independent director, the non-executive directors should meet without the chairman present at least annually to appraise the chairman's performance (as described in A.6.1) and on such other occasions as are deemed appropriate.	Steps Taken									

Code Provision		Compliance	1	-	-	-	-	-	-		1 = "Yes" 0 = "No"
A.1.4	Where directors have concerns which cannot be resolved about the running of the company or a proposed action, they should ensure that their concerns are recorded in the Board minutes.	Steps Taken									
		Compliance	1	-	-	-	-	-	-		1 = "Yes" 0 = "No"
	On resignation, a non-executive director should provide a written statement to the chairman, for circulation to the Board, if they have any such concerns.	Steps Taken									

Code Provision		Compliance	1	-	-	-	-	-	-		1 = "Yes" 0 = "No"
A.1.5	The company should arrange appropriate insurance cover in respect of legal action against its directors.	Steps Taken								2	

RESULTS

		Compliance								
The number of **complete provisions** complied with.	a	Provisions	5	.	.	.	.	.	.	-To Summary sheet
The number of **components** complied with.	b	Components	10	.	.	.	.	.	.	-To Summary sheet

		% Compliance							
Compliance rate for **complete provisions**.	a/c	Provisions	100%	.	.	.	.	.	.
Compliance rate for **components**.	b/d	Components	100%	.	.	.	.	.	.

Figure 11.1 *Continued*

The Chairman and Chief Executive

What is the principle?

There should be a clear division of responsibilities at the head of the company between the running of the Board and the executive responsibility for the running of the company's business. No one individual should have unfettered powers of decision.

Supporting principle

The Chairman is responsible for leadership of the Board, ensuring its effectiveness on all aspects of its role and setting its agenda.

The Chairman is also responsible for ensuring that the directors receive accurate, timely and clear information.

The Chairman should ensure effective communication with shareholders.

The Chairman should also facilitate the effective contribution of Non-Executive Directors (NEDs) in particular and ensure constructive relations between Executive and NEDs.

In plain English?

Running the Board is the Chairman's job. Running the company is the Chief Executive Officer's (CEO's) job. The CEO reports to the Board.

The two jobs act as a natural counterweight to each other, so no one person should have the power of both jobs.

What needs to be done?

If both roles are currently held by one person, split the functions into two distinct roles.

This is a good place to start with NED recruitment, but the Chairman needs to be carefully selected.

Recruiting a NED into the position of Chairman is a high-profile message to the stakeholders that a serious step has been taken in CG.

Components in this section:

Code Provisions	*Reference: Appendix*	*Example/Suggestion for Compliance*
A.2.1 The roles of Chairman and Chief Executive should not be exercised by the same individual.	Appendix 3: The Role of the Chairman	The role of Chairman should be held by an independent NED. The role of Chairman should not be held by the CEO.
The division of responsibilities between the Chairman and Chief Executive should be clearly established, set out in writing and agreed by the Board.	Appendix 4: The Role of the Chief Executive	A list of responsibilities for each role should be agreed by the Board.
A.2.2 The Chairman should on appointment meet the independence criteria set out in A.3.1 below.		Recruit a truly independent Chairman at the outset; not a sinecure
A Chief Executive should not go on to be Chairman of the same company.		A rule to observe.
If exceptionally a Board decides that a Chief Executive should become the Chairman, the Board should consult major shareholders in advance and should set out its reasons to shareholders at the time of the appointment and in the next Annual Report.		

Summary checklists

Things to be created or adopted

- A list of duties for the Chairman.
- A list of duties for the Chief Executive Officer.
- Agreement by the Board for both lists of duties.

Procedures to be created or implemented

- The Chairman should meet the independence criteria on appointment. (specified in Appendices)
- The CEO should not be allowed to go on to become Chairman. If it is decided this should happen (in exceptional circumstances) the major shareholders should be consulted and their agreement sought.

Disclosures to be undertaken

- If the Board decides that the Chairman and CEO should be the same person, this should be explained and justified in the company's Annual Report.
- If the Board decides to appoint the outgoing CEO as the Chairman, an explanation and justification should be outlined in the Annual Report.

See:

Appendix 3: The Role of the Chairman; and
Appendix 4: The Role of the Chief Executive

Score Chart

Figure 12.1 on the following page is a chart for this section of the Code.

Please refer to '*Scoring Chart – ACCEPTS*™ *Method Instructions*' (on page 53).

Following the above instructions, complete this chart first, then transcribe your results to the '*Grand Score Chart*' on page 197.

Excel® spreadsheet

An integrated Excel® spreadsheet model of all the individual score sheets and the *Grand Score Chart* (on page 197) is enclosed with this book.

A	DIRECTORS	Chapter 12
A.2	Chairman & Chief Executive	

Principle: There should be a clear division of responsibilities at the head of the company between the running of the Board and the executive responsibility for the running of the company's business.
No one individual should have unfettered powers of decision.

Code Provision			Date							Appendix	
		Compliance	1	-	-	-	-	-	-		1 = "Yes" 0 = "No"
A.2.1	The roles of chairman and chief executive should not be exercised by the same individual. The division of responsibilities between the chairman and chief executive should be clearly established, set out in writing and agreed by the Board.	Steps Taken								3 4	

Code Provision											
		Compliance	1	-	-	-	-	-	-		1 = "Yes" 0 = "No"
A.2.2	The chairman should on appointment meet the independence criteria set out in A.3.1 below.	Steps Taken									
		Compliance	1	-	-	-	-	-	-		1 = "Yes" 0 = "No"
	A chief executive should not go on to be chairman of the same company. If exceptionally a Board decides that a chief executive should become chairman, the Board should consult major shareholders in advance and should set out its reasons to shareholders at the time of the appointment and in the next Annual Report.	Steps Taken									

RESULTS

		Compliance								
The number of **complete provisions** complied with.	a	Provisions	2	.	.	.	.	.	.	-To Summary sheet
The number of **components** complied with.	b	Components	3	.	.	.	.	.	.	-To Summary sheet

		% Compliance							
Compliance rate for **complete provisions**.	a/c	Provisions	100%	.	.	.	.	.	.
Compliance rate for **components**.	b/d	Components	100%	.	.	.	.	.	.

Figure 12.1

13 Board Balance

What is the principle?

The Board should include a balance of Executive and Non-Executive Directors (and in particular independent Non-Executive Directors) such that no individual or small group of individuals can dominate the Board's decision-making.

Supporting principles

The board should not be so large as to be unwieldy.

The board should be of sufficient size that the balance of skills and experience is appropriate for the requirements of the business and that changes to the Board's composition can be managed without undue disruption.

To ensure that power and information are not concentrated in one or two individuals, there should be a strong presence on the Board of both Executive and Non-Executive Directors.

The value of ensuring that committee membership is refreshed and that undue reliance is not placed on particular individuals should be taken into account in deciding Chairmanship and membership of committees.

No one other than the committee Chairman and members is entitled to be present at a meeting of the Nomination, Audit or Remuneration Committee, but others may attend at the invitation of the committee.

In plain English?

The overall size of the Board should be determined by the complexity of the business, and the balance of skills and experience needed.

The ultimate aim is for a Board that comprises an equal number of Executive Directors and NEDs, plus a NED Chairman.

NEDs should be independent wherever possible, having no direct or indirect connection with the business or other directors.

The purpose of there being balance to the Board appointments is to create objectivity. Decisions should be made, having been subjected to debate by both Executive Directors and experienced NEDs.

A 'Whistle-blowing Procedure' should be adopted. This is seen as good practice to ensure senior management is the first to hear about a scandal, as opposed to the last. It attempts to ensure there *is* a procedure, instead of a member of staff inventing one.

What needs to be done?

As mentioned earlier, the recruitment of NEDs to the Board is crucial.

The CG initiative is heavily diluted in its effect if this is not done.

The expectation of the Code for an equal balance between Executive Directors and NEDs, plus a NED Chairman, is aimed primarily at FTSE 350 companies. This is an ultimate aspiration in Board balance.

Other companies are recommended to have at least two independent NEDs.

The independence of NEDs is important to make this exercise meaningful and useful. It cannot be emphasized enough how beneficial SMEs have found the inclusion of experienced NEDs on their Boards in their success.

To be clear about the criteria for independence, it means a NED:

- has not been an employee in the last 5 years;
- has not had a material business relationship with the company directly;
- has not had a material business relationship with the company indirectly e.g. as a partner, shareholder, director or senior employee of a body that has such a relationship with the company;
- is not paid any inducement beyond the standard directors fees. i.e. no incentive schemes, option plans or pension arrangements;
- has no family ties with the company, directors or advisors;
- has no cross-directorships or links with directors through other companies;
- does not represent any significant shareholder; and
- has not served on the Board for more than 9 years.

Most of these criteria will be obvious. The final point, regarding duration of time, meets the Code's requirement to refresh the Board, preventing stagnation, complacency and ensuring the renewal of skills to the Board.

A senior *NED* should be introduced as the point of contact for a 'Whistle-blowing Procedure'. This is simply a well-publicized procedure within the company to give staff an independent means of reporting actual or intended wrongdoing.

Components in this section:

Code Provisions	*Reference: Appendix*	*Example/Suggestion for Compliance*
A.3.1 The Board should identify in the Annual Report each Non-Executive Director it considers to be independent. The Board should determine whether the director is independent in character and judgment and whether there are relationships or circumstances which are likely to affect, or could appear to affect, the director's judgment. The Board should state its reasons if it determines that a director is independent notwithstanding the existence of relationships or circumstances which may appear relevant to its determination, including if the director:	Appendix 1: Annual Report – CG Disclosures	The Annual Report should list all directors. Against the name of each Executive Director, specify their function (CEO, CFO or FD, etc.). NEDs should be identified. State who is Chairman. State who is Senior NED, the vice-Chairman. State who of the NEDs are independent, based on the criteria specified below:
– has been an employee of the company or group within the last five years;		– NED is not 'independent' because of his familiarity with management.

Continued

Code Provisions		Reference: Appendix	Example/Suggestion for Compliance
A.3.1 (contd.)	– has, or has had within the last three years, a material business relationship with the company either directly, or as a partner, shareholder, director or senior employee of a body that has such a relationship with the company;		– NED is not 'independent' because he may have (or have had) an intimate relationship with the company. Outsiders will not see this NED as objective or independent as he is already 'native'.
	– has received or receives additional remuneration from the company apart from a director's fee, participates in the company's share option or a performance-related pay scheme, or is a member of the company's pension scheme;		– NED is not 'independent' because he has a vested interest in the company's valuation through share options. Being a member of the pension scheme may compromise a NEDs long-term outlook and behaviour.
	– has close family ties with any of the company's advisers, directors or senior employees;		– NED is not 'independent' because there may be personal obligations impeding his judgement.
	– holds cross-directorships or has significant links with other directors through involvement in other companies or bodies		– NED is not 'independent' because there may be the possibility of NEDs accommodating each other in their various companies.
	– represents a significant shareholder; or		– NED is not 'independent' because he cannot be deemed to be acting in the interests of all shareholders.
	– has served on the Board for more than nine years from the date of their first election.		– NED is not 'independent' because close relationships develop over time

Continued

Code Provisions		Reference: Appendix	Example/Suggestion for Compliance
A.3.1 (contd.)			with Executive Directors and senior management, possibly compromising objectivity.
A.3.2	Except for smaller* companies, at least half of the Board, excluding the Chairman, should comprise Non-Executive Directors determined by the Board to be independent. A smaller company should have at least two independent Non-Executive Directors. * companies below the FTSE 350 for full year before the reporting year.		An independent NED Chairman should be appointed as a matter of urgency. Subsequent NED appointments should be made to enhance the Board with candidates with specific skills. It is recommended you look to a 'role model' company (not a competitor) and try to persuade an Executive Director to be a NED for your company. Alternatively, use a head-hunter.
A.3.3	The Board should appoint one of the independent Non-Executive Directors to be the senior independent director. The senior independent director should be available to shareholders if they have concerns which contact through the normal channels of Chairman, Chief Executive or finance director has failed to resolve or for which such contact is inappropriate.		Once a Chairman is in place, a Senior independent NED should be appointed next, to both deputise for the Chairman and perform other functions. The Senior independent NED is a second objective 'port of call' for unhappy shareholders to talk to.

Summary checklists

Things to be created or adopted:

- Filling an appropriate number of independent NED positions to balance against the number of Executive Directors, plus an independent NED Chairman is the ideal, under the Code.
- There is a minimum recommendation of two independent NEDs for all companies outside the FTSE 350.

Procedures to be created or implemented:

- A Whistle-blowing Procedure.

Disclosures to be undertaken

- All NEDs, considered by the Board to be independent, are identified as such in the Annual Report.

See:

Appendix 11: The Whistle-blowing Procedure

Score Chart

Figure 13.1 on the following page is a chart for this section of the Code.

Please refer to *Scoring Chart – ACCEPTS™ Method Instructions* (on page 53)

Following the above instructions, complete this chart first, then transcribe your results to the *Grand Score Chart* on page 197.

Excel® spreadsheet

An integrated Excel® spreadsheet model of all the individual score sheets and the *Grand Score Chart* (on page 197) is enclosed with this book.

A	DIRECTORS	Chapter 13

A.3	Board Balance and Independence

Principle: The Board should include a balance of executive and non-executive directors (and in particular independent non-executive directors) such that no individual or small group of individuals can dominate the Board's decision taking.

Code Provisions

			Date							Appendix	
		Compliance	1	-	-	-	-	-	-		1 = "Yes" 0 = "No"
A.3.1	The Board should identify in the Annual Report each non-executive director it considers to be independent. The Board should determine whether the director is independent in character and judgment and whether there are relationships or circumstances which are likely to affect, or could appear to affect, the director's judgment. The Board should state its reasons if it determines that a director is independent notwithstanding the existence of relationships or circumstances which may appear relevant to its determination, including if the director:	Steps Taken								1	
		Compliance	1	-	-	-	-	-	-		1 = "Yes" 0 = "No"
	- has been an employee of the company or group within the last five years;	Steps Taken									
		Compliance	1	-	-	-	-	-	-		1 = "Yes" 0 = "No"
	- has, or has had within the last three years, a material business relationship with the company either directly, or as a partner, shareholder, director or senior employee of a body that has such a relationship with the company;	Steps Taken									
		Compliance	1	-	-	-	-	-	-		1 = "Yes" 0 = "No"
	- has received or receives additional remuneration from the company apart from a director's fee, participates in the company's share option or a performance-related pay scheme, or is a member of the company's pension scheme;	Steps Taken									
		Compliance	1	-	-	-	-	-	-		1 = "Yes" 0 = "No"
	- has close family ties with any of the company's advisers, directors or senior employees;	Steps Taken									
		Compliance	1	-	-	-	-	-	-		1 = "Yes" 0 = "No"
	- holds cross-directorships or has significant links with other directors through involvement in other companies or bodies;	Steps Taken									

Figure 13.1

Code	Provision										
		Compliance	1	-	-	-	-	-	-		1 = "Yes" 0 = "No"
	- represents a significant shareholder; or	Steps Taken									
		Compliance	1	-	-	-	-	-	-		1 = "Yes" 0 = "No"
	- has served on the Board for more than nine years from the date of their first election.	Steps Taken									

Code Provision

Code	Provision										
		Compliance	1	-	-	-	-	-	-		1 = "Yes" 0 = "No"
A.3.2	Except for smaller* companies, at least half the Board, excluding the chairman, should comprise non-executive directors determined by the Board to be independent. A smaller company should have at least two independent non-executive directors. * companies below the FTSE 350 for full year before the reporting year.	Steps Taken									

Code Provision

Code	Provision										
		Compliance	1	-	-	-	-	-	-		1 = "Yes" 0 = "No"
A.3.3	The Board should appoint one of the independent non-executive directors to be the senior independent director.	Steps Taken									
		Compliance	1	-	-	-	-	-	-		1 = "Yes" 0 = "No"
	The senior independent director should be available to shareholders if they have concerns which contact through the normal channels of chairman, chief executive or finance director has failed to resolve or for which such contact is inappropriate.	Steps Taken								5	

RESULTS

		Compliance								
The number of **complete provisions** complied with.	a	Provisions	3	.	.	.	.	.	.	-To Summary sheet
The number of **components** complied with.	b	Components	11	.	.	.	.	.	.	-To Summary sheet

		% Compliance							
Compliance rate for **complete provisions**.	a/c	Provisions	100%	.	.	.	.	.	.
Compliance rate for **components**.	b/d	Components	100%	.	.	.	.	.	.

Figure 13.1 *Continued*

Board Appointments

What is the principle?

There should be a formal, rigorous and transparent procedure for the appointment of new directors to the Board.

Supporting principles

Appointments to the Board should be made on merit and against objective criteria.

Care should be taken to ensure that appointees have enough time available to devote to the job. This is particularly important in the case of Chairmanships.

The Board should satisfy itself that plans are in place for orderly succession for appointments to the Board and to the senior management, so as to maintain an appropriate balance of skills and experience within the company and on the Board.

In plain English?

An appointment to the Board should be made with a view to engaging the right person, based on proper, objective criteria. The primary consideration is merit – can the appointee do the job?

The Board should form a Nomination Committee to take care of the recruitment process, making recommendations to the full Board of its selections.

The Nomination Committee is an objective body.

What needs to be done?

The independent NEDs should be appointed to this committee at the earliest opportunity, until all members of the Nomination Committee are NEDs and the only Executive Director member is the CEO.

Components in this section:

Code Provisions	*Reference: Appendix*	*Example/Suggestion for Compliance*
A.4.1 There should be a Nomination Committee that should lead the process for Board appointments and make recommendations to the Board.	Appendix 12: Nomination Committee – Terms of Reference	Appoint independent NEDs to this Committee as they are recruited. This Committee becomes the gatekeeper of who sits on the Board. New appointments will only be made on the basis of talent and ability.
A majority of members of the Nomination Committee should be independent Non-Executive Directors.		Aside from the CEO, there should be no Executive Directors on this Committee.
The Chairman or an independent Non-Executive Director should chair the committee, but the Chairman should not chair the Nomination Committee when it is dealing with the appointment of a successor to the Chairmanship.		The Chairman of the Board should not be the Chairman of the Nomination Committee, in order to comply with the Code and the ICSA guidelines. It should be another independent NED. (Particularly so when dealing with the Chairman's successor.)
The Nomination Committee should make available its terms of reference, explaining its role and the authority delegated to it by the Board.	Appendix 1: Annual Report – CG Disclosures	The policy and terms of reference should be disclosed in the Annual Report.

Continued

Code Provisions	*Reference: Appendix*	*Example/Suggestion for Compliance*
A.4.2 The Nomination Committee should evaluate the balance of skills, knowledge and experience on the Board and, in the light of this evaluation, prepare a description of the role and capabilities required for a particular appointment.		The Nomination Committee should look for gaps in the experience and skills available on the Board. It should create the specification of the person to fill that role.
A.4.3 For the appointment of a Chairman, the Nomination Committee should prepare a job specification, including an assessment of the time commitment expected, recognizing the need for availability in the event of crises.		When appointing a Chairman to the Board, the Nomination Committee should create a clear job specification and make certain the candidates to be considered can afford the time to do the job.
A Chairman's other significant commitments should be disclosed to the Board before appointment and included in the Annual Report. Changes to such commitments should be reported to the Board as they arise, and included in the next Annual Report.	Appendix 1: Annual Report – CG Disclosures	A disclosure item.
No individual should be appointed to a second Chairmanship of a FTSE 100 company.		Rule. Disclose if breached.

Continued

Code Provisions	Reference: Appendix	Example/Suggestion for Compliance
A.4.4 The terms and conditions of appointment of Non-Executive Directors should be made available for inspection (for 15 minutes prior to and during the AGM).		NED service contracts (or terms and conditions of appointment) should be available for inspection by shareholders.
The letter of appointment should set out the expected time commitment.		NEDs will have other business commitments.
Non-Executive Directors should undertake that they will have sufficient time to meet what is expected of them.		It is vital that the Nomination Committee establish that any NEDs who are recruited to the Board are able to give the time to meet their agreed commitments.
Their other significant commitments should be disclosed to the Board before appointment, with a broad indication of the time involved and the Board should be informed of subsequent changes.		The Nomination Committee should be conscious of any changes to the NEDs' commitments.
A.4.5 The Board should not agree to a full-time Executive Director taking on more than one Non-Executive Directorship in a FTSE 100 company nor the Chairmanship of such a company.		An Executive Director should not become a NED on the Board of more than one listed company. An Executive Director should not become Chairman of the Board of a listed company.

Continued

Code Provisions	*Reference: Appendix*	*Example/Suggestion for Compliance*
A.4.6 A separate section of the Annual Report should describe the work of the Nomination Committee, including the process it has used in relation to Board appointments. An explanation should be given if neither an external search consultancy nor open advertising has been used in the appointment of a Chairman or a Non-Executive Director.	Appendix 1: Annual Report – CG Disclosures	There is no point in putting this Committee in place if you don't explain what it is, what it does and who is in it! To ensure the Nomination Committee acts objectively, it should explain in the Annual Report if it appoints NEDs without the use of external advertising or head-hunters.

Summary checklists

Things to be created or adopted

- Nomination Committee.
- The terms of reference of the Nomination Committee.
- A Chairman of the Nomination Committee.

Procedures to be created or implemented

- Schedule regular meetings of the Nomination Committee principally to:
  - Review current Board skills and NED composition
  - Recommend required Board skills and NEDs
  - Prepare job descriptions for proposed new appointments
  - Concern itself with succession planning
  - Ensure NED appointees have adequate time to perform duties
  - Recommend rotation and re-election (or not) of Directors
- Chairman of the Nomination Committee should be available at the AGM to answer any questions from shareholders.

Disclosures to be undertaken

- Annual Report disclosures of:
  - Brief terms of reference and authority of the Committee
  - Composition of the Nomination Committee (Chairman and members)
  - Frequency of meetings
  - Attendance of Committee members
  - Reasons why a Director(s) should be re-appointed at the next Annual General Meeting

See:

Appendix 7: Chairman of the Nomination Committee – Job Description; and
Appendix 12: Nomination Committee – Terms of Reference

Score Chart

Figure 14.1 on the following page is a chart for this section of the Code.

Please refer to *Scoring Chart – ACCEPTS™ Method* Instructions (on page 53)

Following the above instructions, complete this chart first, then transcribe your results to the *Grand Score Chart* on page 197.

Excel® spreadsheet

An integrated Excel® spreadsheet model of all the individual score sheets and the *Grand Score Chart* (on page 197) is enclosed with this book.

A	DIRECTORS	Chapter 14
A.4	Appointments To The Board	

Principle: There should be a formal, rigorous and transparent procedure for the appointment of new directors to the Board.

Code Provisions

Ref	Provision		Date							Appendix	
A.4.1		Compliance	1	-	-	-	-	-	-		1 = "Yes" 0 = "No"
	There should be a Nomination Committee which should lead the process for Board appointments and make recommendations to the Board.	Steps Taken								12	
		Compliance	1	-	-	-	-	-	-		1 = "Yes" 0 = "No"
	A majority of members of the Nomination Committee should be independent non-executive directors.	Steps Taken								12	
		Compliance	1	-	-	-	-	-	-		1 = "Yes" 0 = "No"
	The chairman or an independent non-executive director should chair the committee, but the chairman should not chair the Nomination Committee when it is dealing with the appointment of a successor to the chairmanship.	Steps Taken								7	
		Compliance	1	-	-	-	-	-	-		1 = "Yes" 0 = "No"
	The Nomination Committee should make available its terms of reference, explaining its role and the authority delegated to it by the Board.	Steps Taken								6	

Code Provision

Ref	Provision		Date							Appendix	
A.4.2		Compliance	1	-	-	-	-	-	-		1 = "Yes" 0 = "No"
	The Nomination Committee should evaluate the balance of skills, knowledge and experience on the Board and, in the light of this evaluation, prepare a description of the role and capabilities required for a particular appointment.	Steps Taken								12	

Figure 14.1

Code Provision											
		Compliance	1	-	-	-	-	-	-		1 = "Yes" 0 = "No"
A.4.3	For the appointment of a chairman, the Nomination Committee should prepare a job specification, including an assessment of the time commitment expected, recognising the need for availability in the event of crises.	Steps Taken								7	
		Compliance	1	-	-	-	-	-	-		1 = "Yes" 0 = "No"
	A chairman's other significant commitments should be disclosed to the Board before appointment and included in the Annual Report. Changes to such commitments should be reported to the Board as they arise, and included in the next Annual Report.	Steps Taken									
		Compliance	1	-	-	-	-	-	-		1 = "Yes" 0 = "No"
	No individual should be appointed to a second chairmanship of a FTSE 100 company.	Steps Taken									

Code Provision											
		Compliance	1	-	-	-	-	-	-		1 = "Yes" 0 = "No"
A.4.4	The terms and conditions of appointment of non-executive directors should be made available for inspection. *(for 15 minutes prior to and during the AGM).*	Steps Taken									
		Compliance	1	-	-	-	-	-	-		1 = "Yes" 0 = "No"
	The letter of appointment should set out the expected time commitment. Non-executive directors should undertake that they will have sufficient time to meet what is expected of them. Their other significant commitments should be disclosed to the Board before appointment, with a broad indication of the time involved and the Board should be informed of subsequent changes.	Steps Taken								6	

Code Provision											
		Compliance	1	-	-	-	-	-	-		1 = "Yes" 0 = "No"
A.4.5	The Board should not agree to a full time executive director taking on more than one non-executive directorship in a FTSE 100 company nor the chairmanship of such a company.	Steps Taken									

Figure 14.1 *Continued*

Code Provision										
		Compliance	1	-	-	-	-	-		1 = "Yes" 0 = "No"
A.4.6	A separate section of the Annual Report should describe the work of the Nomination Committee, including the process it has used in relation to Board appointments. An explanation should be given if neither an external search consultancy nor open advertising has been used in the appointment of a chairman or a non-executive director.	Steps Taken							1	

RESULTS										
		Compliance								
The number of **complete provisions** complied with.	a	Provisions	6	.	.	.	.	.	.	-To Summary sheet
The number of **components** complied with.	b	Components	12	.	.	.	.	.	.	-To Summary sheet
		% Compliance								
Compliance rate for **complete provisions**.	a/c	Provisions	100%	.	.	.	.	.	.	
Compliance rate for **components**.	b/d	Components	100%	.	.	.	.	.	.	

Figure 14.1 *Continued*

Board Information

What is the principle?

The Board should be supplied in a timely manner with information in a form and of a quality appropriate to enable it to discharge its duties. All directors should receive induction on joining the Board and should regularly update and refresh their skills and knowledge.

Supporting principles

The Chairman is responsible for ensuring that the directors receive accurate, timely and clear information.

Management has an obligation to provide such information but directors should seek clarification or amplification where necessary.

The Chairman should ensure that the directors continually update their skills and the knowledge and familiarity with the company required to fulfil their role both on the Board and on Board committees.

The company should provide the necessary resources for developing and updating its directors' knowledge and capabilities.

Under the direction of the Chairman, the Company Secretary's responsibilities include ensuring good information flows within the Board.

The Company Secretary should be responsible for advising the Board through the Chairman on all governance matters.

In plain English?

The Board should have the latest and best information available to help it make its decisions.

New directors should be thoroughly familiarized with all aspects of the company.

All directors are obliged to keep their skills and knowledge current.

The Company Secretary is the officer responsible for ensuring Board compliance. The Chairman should include these matters in the induction of new directors, and all directors should have access to the Company Secretary for advice on compliance issues.

What needs to be done?

A regular reporting cycle should be adopted within the company.

All Board agenda items should be accompanied by written papers, where possible.

All Board papers should be circulated to directors in good time for them to be understood and digested. This allows for meaningful discussions to take place and meaningful decisions to be made.

On induction of a new director, the Chairman should tailor the induction programme making full use of the Company Secretary, particularly in the formal processes of the Board.

Where training is required, whether for new or existing directors, this should be provided at the company's expense. Similarly, when professional, independent, external advice is required, this should also be at the company's expense.

This will ensure that properly informed decisions are taken.

All Board committees should be adequately resourced under the same principle.

Major shareholders should be given the opportunity to meet new directors – particularly NEDs.

The Company Secretary should be available to all directors regarding matters of Board procedure.

As the Board's compliance officer, the appointment and removal of the Company Secretary should become a matter for the entire Board.

Components in this section:

Code Provisions	*Reference: Appendix*	*Example/Suggestion for Compliance*
A.5.1 The Chairman should ensure that new directors receive a full, formal and tailored induction on joining the Board.		The Chairman should make full use of the Company Secretary in preparing each individual induction of new directors.

Continued

Code Provisions		*Reference: Appendix*	*Example/Suggestion for Compliance*
A.5.1 (contd.)	As part of this, the company should offer to major shareholders the opportunity to meet a new Non-Executive Director.		Most SMEs should be able to arrange the introduction of the new NEDs to their major shareholders.
A.5.2	The Board should ensure that directors, especially Non-Executive Directors, have access to independent professional advice at the company's expense where they judge it necessary to discharge their responsibilities as directors. Committees should be provided with sufficient resources to undertake their duties.		All directors should make full use of the Company Secretary in acquiring information. Independent professional advice and training should be obtained, when necessary, at the company's expense. Each Committee should be adequately supported by the company, financially and in manpower.
A.5.3	All directors should have access to the advice and services of the Company Secretary, who is responsible to the Board for ensuring that Board procedures are complied with. Both the appointment and removal of the Company Secretary should be a matter for the Board as a whole.		The Company Secretary is responsible for ensuring the Board complies with proper procedures. Any queries from directors on these matters should be made to the Company Secretary directly. A further objectivity issue. Given that the Company Secretary is the Board compliance officer, insisting on his appointment or removal being a Board matter ensures that no one director can remove him for reasons of convenience.

Summary checklists

Things to be created or adopted

- Where possible, each Board agenda item should be accompanied by a Board paper.
- A planner for Board meetings should also include a latest date for circulation of Board papers (One or two weeks before the meeting).

Procedures to be created or implemented

- Circulation of agenda and Board papers in good time for the Board meeting.
- Directors should take independent advice, as necessary, at the company's expense.
- Directors should undertake training, as necessary, at the company's expense.
- The Company Secretary should be responsible for Board procedures, and be available to all directors for advice on such matters.

Disclosures to be undertaken

- None.

See:

Appendix 15: CG Role of the Company Secretary

Score Chart

Figure 15.1 on the following page is a chart for this section of the Code.

Please refer to *Scoring Chart – ACCEPTS™ Method Instructions* (on page 53).

Following the above instructions, complete this chart first, then transcribe your results to the *Grand Score Chart* on page 197.

Excel® spreadsheet

An integrated Excel® spreadsheet model of all the individual score sheets and the *Grand Score Chart* (on page 197) is enclosed with this book.

A	DIRECTORS	Chapter 15

A.5	Information and Professional Development

Principle: The Board should be supplied in a timely manner with information in a form and of a quality appropriate to enable it to discharge its duties. All directors should receive induction on joining the Board and should regularly update and refresh their skills and knowledge.

Code Provisions			Date							Appendix	
		Compliance	1	-	-	-	-	-	-		1 = "Yes" 0 = "No"
A.5.1	The chairman should ensure that new directors receive a full, formal and tailored induction on joining the Board. As part of this, the company should offer to major shareholders the opportunity to meet a new non-executive director.	Steps Taken									

Code Provision											
		Compliance	1	-	-	-	-	-	-		1 = "Yes" 0 = "No"
A.5.2	The Board should ensure that directors, especially non-executive directors,have access to independent professional advice at the company's expense where they judge it necessary to discharge their responsibilities as directors. Committees should be provided with sufficient resources to undertake their duties.	Steps Taken									

Code Provision											
		Compliance	1	-	-	-	-	-	-		1 = "Yes" 0 = "No"
A.5.3	All directors should have access to the advice and services of the company secretary, who is responsible to the Board for ensuring that Board procedures are complied with. Both the appointment and removal of the company secretary should be a matter for the Board as a whole.	Steps Taken								15	

RESULTS

		Compliance								
The number of **complete provisions** complied with.	a	Provisions	3	.	.	.	.	.	.	-To Summary sheet
The number of **components** complied with.	b	Components	3	.	.	.	.	.	.	-To Summary sheet

		% Compliance							
Compliance rate for **complete provisions**.	a/c	Provisions	100%	.	.	.	.	.	.
Compliance rate for **components**.	b/d	Components	100%	.	.	.	.	.	.

Figure 15.1

16 Board Performance Evaluation

What is the principle?

The Board should undertake a formal and rigorous annual evaluation of its own performance and that of its committees and individual directors.

Supporting principles

Individual evaluation should aim to show whether each director continues to contribute effectively and to demonstrate commitment to the role (including commitment of time for Board and committee meetings and any other duties).

The Chairman should act on the results of the performance evaluation by recognizing the strengths and addressing the weaknesses of the Board and, wherever appropriate, proposing new members be appointed to the Board or seeking the resignation of directors.

In plain English?

The Annual Report should tell the shareholders how the performance evaluation of the Board has been done.

What needs to be done?

Formal Annual Reviews of Executive Directors, usually by CEO.
Formal Annual Reviews of NEDs by the Chairman.
Formal Annual Reviews of Chairman, usually by NEDs, led by the Senior NED.

Components in this section:

Code provisions	*Reference: Appendix*	*Example/Suggestion for Compliance*
A.6.1 The Board should state in the Annual Report how performance evaluation of the Board, its committees	Appendix 10: Performance Evaluation Guidance	The Annual Report should comment to this effect. Executive Directors are frequently evaluated by the CEO.

Continued

Code Provisions		*Reference Appendix*	*Example/Suggestion for Compliance*
A.6.1 (contd.)	and its individual directors has been conducted.		
	The Non-Executive Directors, led by the senior independent director, should be responsible for performance evaluation of the Chairman, taking into account the views of the Executive Directors.		NEDs should be evaluated by the Chairman and the Chairman by the Senior NED, with views from Executive Directors.

Summary checklists

Things to be created or adopted

- None.

Procedures to be created or implemented

- Annual Review of Executive Directors by CEO.
- Annual Review of NEDs by Chairman.
- Annual Review of Chairman, by NEDs. The Senior NED should lead this, taking the views of Executive Directors into account.

Disclosures to be undertaken

- The Board should state in the Annual Report how the performance evaluation of the Board, its committees and its individual directors has been conducted.

See:

Appendix 1: Annual Report – CG Disclosures; and
Appendix 10: Performance Evaluation Guidance.

Score Chart

Figure 16.1 on the following page is a chart for this section of the Code.

Please refer to *Scoring Chart – ACCEPTS™ Method Instructions* (on page 53).

Following the above instructions, complete this chart first, then transcribe your results to the *Grand Score Chart* on page 197.

Excel® spreadsheet

An integrated Excel® spreadsheet model of all the individual score sheets and the *Grand Score Chart* (on page 197) is enclosed with this book.

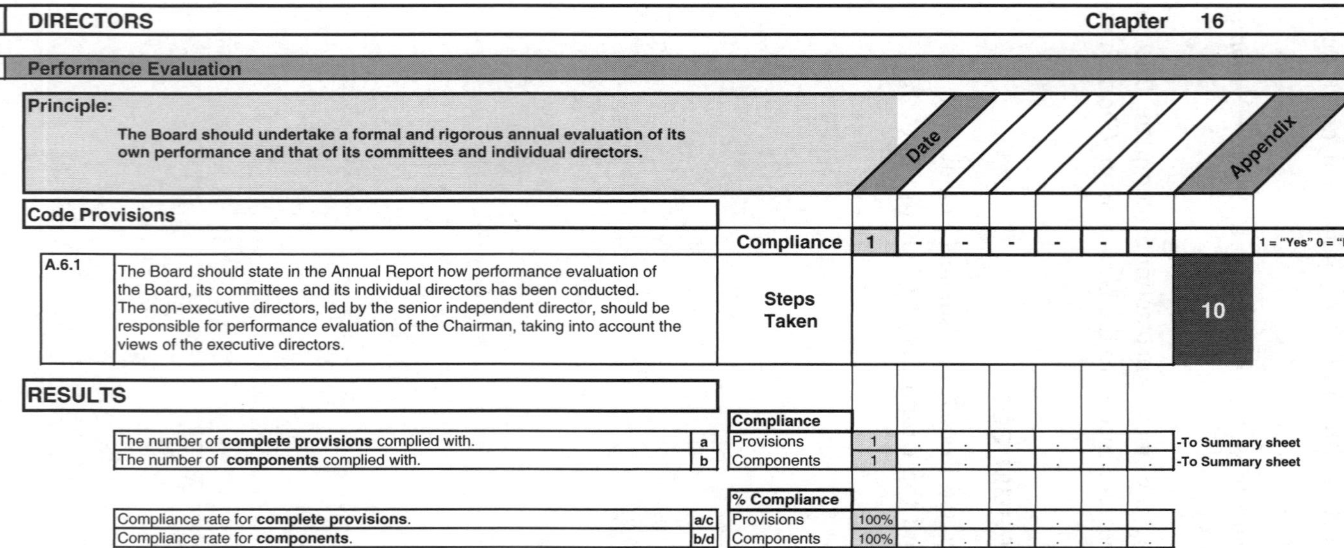

A	DIRECTORS	Chapter 16
A.6	Performance Evaluation	

Principle:

The Board should undertake a formal and rigorous annual evaluation of its own performance and that of its committees and individual directors.

Code Provisions

			Date							Appendix	
		Compliance	1	-	-	-	-	-	-		1 = "Yes" 0 = "No"
A.6.1	The Board should state in the Annual Report how performance evaluation of the Board, its committees and its individual directors has been conducted. The non-executive directors, led by the senior independent director, should be responsible for performance evaluation of the Chairman, taking into account the views of the executive directors.	**Steps Taken**								10	

RESULTS

		Compliance								
The number of **complete provisions** complied with.	a	Provisions	1	.	.	.	.	.	.	-To Summary sheet
The number of **components** complied with.	b	Components	1	.	.	.	.	.	.	-To Summary sheet

		% Compliance							
Compliance rate for **complete provisions**.	a/c	Provisions	100%	.	.	.	.	.	.
Compliance rate for **components**.	b/d	Components	100%	.	.	.	.	.	.

Figure 16.1

Board Re-election

What is the principle?

All directors should be submitted for re-election at regular intervals, subject to continued satisfactory performance. The Board should ensure planned and progressive refreshing of the Board.

Supporting principles

None stated.

The 'too-obvious-to-mention' supporting principle is that of shareholder democracy and the right of the shareholders to decide who runs their business on their behalf.

In a major quoted plc this is only of theoretical significance. This is because individual shareholders normally wield so little power.

In the Small and Medium-sized Enterprise (SME) arena, this is of much more significance as shareholder power is frequently concentrated in fewer hands.

In plain English?

A newly appointed director should be subjected to election by shareholders at the next possible Annual General Meeting (AGM) after appointment. After this, the director should submit to re-election at AGM at least every three years.

Biographical details should accompany election/re-election notices to shareholders.

NEDs should be appointed for a specified term (possibly 3 years), and re-election should *not* be automatic. The Chairman should state a successful review of the NED's performance has taken place when proposing a NED for re-election to another term.

Renewal after six years may well compromise the independence of a NED.

All of these tasks should be considered by the Nomination Committee.

What needs to be done?

Put newly appointed directors forward for shareholder approval at the earliest AGM opportunity.

Put all directors on a three-year cycle of re-election.

Create biographical data for all directors and keep it updated.

Board and Committee performance should be reviewed regularly.

Ensure that the Chairman is rigorous regarding the re-appointment of NEDs to avoid NED independence being compromised through familiarity. If this is not done, the Board will not meet the spirit of the Code, which places importance on 'refreshing' the Board, which it fears may also stagnate.

'Turnover' of NEDs can ensure the inclusion of new skills, as well as removing old skills and maintaining independence.

Components in this section:

Code Provisions		*Reference: Appendix*	*Example/Suggestion for Compliance*
A.7.1	All directors should be subjected to election by shareholders at the first annual general meeting after their appointment, and to re-election thereafter at intervals of no more than three years.	Appendix 5: Guidance on the Role of Non-Executive Director Appendix 6: Sample Letter of Non-Executive Director Appointment	After appointment, a director should be subjected to election by shareholders at the first possible AGM. Thereafter, a director should submit to re-election every three years.
	The names of directors submitted for election or re-election should be accompanied by sufficient biographical		When a director goes before shareholders for election or re-election at AGM, some biographical

Continued

Code Provisions	Reference: Appendix	Example/Suggestion for Compliance
A.7.1 (contd.) details and any other relevant information to enable shareholders to take an informed decision on their election.		background should be presented to the shareholders to help them.
A.7.2 Non-Executive Directors should be appointed for specified terms subject to re-election and to Companies Acts provisions relating to the removal of a director. The Board should set out to shareholders in the papers accompanying a resolution to elect a Non-Executive Director why they believe an individual should be elected.	Appendix 12: Nomination Committee – Terms of Reference	A NED should be appointed for a three-year term. The election papers to shareholders should include the Board's reasons for proposing the NED.
The Chairman should confirm to shareholders when proposing re-election that, following formal performance evaluation, the individual's performance continues to be effective and to demonstrate commitment to the role.	Appendix 1: Annual Report – CG Disclosures	If a NED is to be re-elected for a second term, the Chairman should justify this by telling the shareholders that a formal performance review has taken place. The Chairman should add that the NED's performance 'continues to be effective' and 'demonstrates commitment to the role'.
Any term beyond six years (e.g. two three-year terms) for a Non-Executive Director should be subject to	See page 80.	If a NED is to be re-elected *beyond* a second term, a rigorous review should take place.

Continued

Code Provisions		*Reference: Appendix*	*Example/Suggestion for Compliance*
A.7.2 (contd.)	particularly rigorous review, and should take into account the need for progressive refreshing of the Board. Non-Executive Directors may serve longer than nine years (e.g. three three-year terms), subject to annual re-election. Serving more than nine years could be relevant to the determination of a Non-Executive Director's independence (as set out in provision A.3.1).		This goes against the 'progressive refreshing of the Board' sought by the Code. NEDs may serve longer than 9 years, but doing so may contravene the definition of 'independent'. In other words, a NED may no longer be deemed an independent NED

Summary checklists

Things to be created or adopted

- An annual Director Re-election Planner.
- Biographical background of each director.

Procedures to be created or implemented

- A new director should face election at the first possible AGM.
- All directors should face re-election at AGM every 3 years.
- A NED performance review prior to NED re-election.
- Chairman of the Nomination Committee should be available at the AGM to answer any questions from shareholders.

Disclosures to be undertaken

- Annual Report disclosures of:
  - Brief terms of reference and authority of the Committee;
  - Composition of the Nomination Committee (Chairman & members);
  - Frequency of meetings;
  - Attendance of Committee members;
  - The Board and Committees have been subjected to performance review;

– A NED performance review has been successfully undertaken, prior to the re-election of any NED. Chairman's statement of continuing effectiveness.

See:

Chapter 14: Board Appointments;
Appendix 5: Guidance on the Role of Non-Executive Director;
Appendix 6: Sample Letter of Non-Executive Director Appointment;
Appendix 7: Chairman of the Nomination Committee – Job Description; and
Appendix 12: Nomination Committee – Terms of Reference.

Score Chart

Figure 17.1 on the following page is a chart for this section of the Code.

Please refer to *Scoring Chart – ACCEPTS™ Method Instructions* (on page 53).

Following the above instructions, complete this chart first, then transcribe your results to the *Grand Score Chart* on page 197.

Excel® spreadsheet

An integrated Excel® spreadsheet model of all the individual score sheets and the *Grand Score Chart* (on page 197) is enclosed with this book.

A	DIRECTORS										Chapter 17
A.7	Re-election										
Principle:	All directors should be submitted for re-election at regular intervals, subject to continued satisfactory performance. The Board should ensure planned and progressive refreshing of the Board.		Date							Appendix	
Code Provisions											
A.7.1	All directors should be subject to election by shareholders at the first annual general meeting after their appointment, and to re-election thereafter at intervals of no more than three years.	Compliance	1	-	-	-	-	-	-		1 = "Yes" 0 = "No"
		Steps Taken									
	The names of directors submitted for election or re-election should be accompanied by sufficient biographical details and any other relevant information to enable shareholders to take an informed decision on their election.	Compliance	1	-	-	-	-	-	-		1 = "Yes" 0 = "No"
		Steps Taken									

Figure 17.1

Code Provision											
		Compliance	1	-	-	-	-	-	-		1 = "Yes" 0 = "No"
A.7.2	Non-executive directors should be appointed for specified terms subject to re-election and to Companies Acts provisions relating to the removal of a director. The Board should set out to shareholders in the papers accompanying a resolution to elect a non-executive director why they believe an individual should be elected.	Steps Taken									
		Compliance	1	-	-	-	-	-	-		1 = "Yes" 0 = "No"
	The chairman should confirm to shareholders when proposing re-election that, following formal performance evaluation, the individual's performance continues to be effective and to demonstrate commitment to the role.	Steps Taken									
		Compliance	1	-	-	-	-	-	-		1 = "Yes" 0 = "No"
	Any term beyond six years (e.g. two three-year terms) for a non-executive director should be subject to particularly rigorous review, and should take into account the need for progressive refreshing of the Board. Non-executive directors may serve longer than nine years (e.g. three three-year terms), subject to annual re-election. Serving more than nine years could be relevant to the determination of a non-executive director's independence (as set out in provision A.3.1).	Steps Taken									

RESULTS										
		Compliance								
The number of **complete provisions** complied with.	a	Provisions	2	.	.	.	.	.	.	-To Summary sheet
The number of **components** complied with.	b	Components	5	.	.	.	.	.	.	-To Summary sheet
		% Compliance								
Compliance rate for **complete provisions**.	a/c	Provisions	100%	.	.	.	.	.	.	
Compliance rate for **components**.	b/d	Components	100%	.	.	.	.	.	.	

Figure 17.1 *Continued*

18 Board – Rewards

(a) Level and Make-Up

What is the principle?

Levels of remuneration should be sufficient to attract, retain and motivate directors of the quality required to run the company successfully, but a company should avoid paying more than is necessary for this purpose. A significant proportion of Executive Directors' remuneration should be structured so as to link rewards to corporate and individual performance.

Supporting principle

The Remuneration Committee should judge where to position their company relative to other companies. But they should use such comparisons with caution, in view of the risk of an upward ratchet of remuneration levels with no corresponding improvement in performance.

They should also be sensitive to pay and employment conditions elsewhere in the group, especially when determining annual salary increments.

In plain English?

Reward packages for the Board should be made with a view of paying the right amount, based on proper objective criteria.

This needs to be adequate to attract and retain capable directors, as well as providing motivation to excel. Care should be taken to avoid paying too much.

The Board should form a Remuneration Committee to take responsibility for the reward process, making recommendations to the full Board.

What needs to be done?

The independent NEDs should be appointed to this committee at the earliest opportunity, until the majority of members of the Remuneration Committee are NEDs.

The only Executive Director member is the CEO, who may not take part in discussions on his own remuneration package.

A significant proportion of the total remuneration paid to each Executive Director should become performance-related. The key principle is that the performance-related element should mirror the success of the company.

Added note

The design of the performance-related remuneration system is a major area in CG. There are specific rules in *Schedule A* of the Code. These are:

- The Remuneration Committee should consider whether the directors should be eligible for annual bonuses. If so, performance conditions should be relevant, stretching and designed to enhance shareholder value. Upper limits should be set and disclosed. There may be a case for part payment in shares to be held for a significant period.
- The Remuneration Committee should consider whether the directors should be eligible for benefits under long-term incentive schemes.
  Traditional share option schemes should be weighed against other kinds of long-term incentive scheme.
  In normal circumstances, shares granted or other forms of deferred remuneration should not vest, and options should not be exercisable, in less than three years.
  Directors should be encouraged to hold their shares for a further period after vesting or exercise, subject to the need to finance any costs of acquisition and associated tax liabilities.
- Any new long-term incentive schemes which are proposed should be approved by shareholders and should preferably replace any existing schemes or at least form part of a well-considered overall plan, incorporating existing schemes. The total rewards potentially available should not be excessive.
- Payouts or grants under all incentive schemes, including new grants under existing share option schemes, should be subject to challenging performance criteria reflecting the company's objectives. Consideration should be given to criteria which reflect the company's performance relative to a group of comparator

companies in some key variables such as total shareholder return.

- Grants under executive share option and other long-term incentive schemes should normally be phased rather than awarded in one large block.
- In general, only basic salary should be pensionable.
- The Remuneration Committee should consider the pension consequences and associated costs to the company of basic salary increases and any other changes in pensionable remuneration, especially for directors close to retirement.

Components in this section:

Code Provisions	*Reference: Appendix*	*Example/Suggestion for Compliance*
B.1.1 The performance-related elements of remuneration should form a significant proportion of the total remuneration package of Executive Directors and should be designed to align their interests with those of shareholders and to give these directors keen incentives to perform at the highest levels.		It is important to align the success of the company with the rewards of the Executive Directors. To maximize motivation, performance-related elements of remuneration package should be a significant proportion of total remuneration packages.
In designing schemes of performance-related remuneration, the Remuneration Committee should follow the provisions in Schedule A to this Code.		See above for the rules to Schedule A.
B.1.2 Executive share options should not be offered at a discount, save as permitted by the relevant provisions of the Listing Rules.		Share Options offered at a discount produce an instant profit for no performance. Therefore, they are discouraged.

Continued

Code Provisions		Reference: Appendix	Example/Suggestion for Compliance
B.1.3	Levels of remuneration for Non-Executive Directors should reflect the time commitment and responsibilities of the role.		NEDs are normally paid a basic fee. There may be a 'consultancy rate' for days worked beyond contract. NEDs who are on Audit Committees may be paid a little more.
	Remuneration for Non-Executive Directors should not include share options. If, exceptionally, options are granted, shareholder approval should be sought in advance and any shares acquired by exercise of the options should be held until at least one year after the Non-Executive Director leaves the Board. Holding of share options could be relevant to the determination of a Non-Executive Director's independence (as set out in provision A.3.1).	See page 80	Share options should not be offered to NEDs without shareholder approval. If share options are offered, they should be held until at least one year after the NED leaves the Board. Share options may be deemed to compromise the independence of a NED.
B.1.4	Where a company releases an Executive Director to serve as a Non-Executive Director elsewhere, the remuneration report should include a statement as to whether or not the director will retain such earnings and, if so, what the remuneration is.		If an Executive Director also has a NED position elsewhere and he is paid, these earnings should be declared in the Annual Report.

Continued

Code Provisions		Reference: Appendix	Example/Suggestion for Compliance
B.1.5	The Remuneration Committee should carefully consider what compensation commitments (including pension contributions and all other elements) their directors' terms of appointment would entail in the event of early termination. The aim should be to avoid rewarding poor performance. They should take a robust line on reducing compensation to reflect departing directors' obligations to mitigate loss.		The Remuneration Committee should avoid generous compensation in the event of the company terminating a director's contract. Payment for failure is particularly unpalatable to shareholders under any guise, whether it is a termination bonus or additional pension contributions.
B.1.6	Notice or contract periods should be set at one year or less. If it is necessary to offer longer notice or contract periods to new directors recruited from outside, such periods should reduce to one year or less after the initial period.		No director should be eligible for more than one year's compensation for early contract termination.

Summary checklists

Things to be created or adopted

- The Remuneration Committee.
- The Terms of Reference of the Remuneration Committee.
- A Chairman of the Remuneration Committee.

- A Remuneration Policy for the company, regarding Executive Directors and NEDs.
- A coherent and self-funding bonus plan for Executive Directors.

Procedures to be created or implemented

- A significant proportion of each Executive Director's Remuneration package should become bonus-related.
- Executive Director's bonuses should be aligned to a success metric of the company.
- No share options should be offered to Executive Directors at a discount.
- No service or employment contracts should be offered to directors that exceed one year.
- No share options should be offered to NEDs unless shareholders approve. Even if they do approve, NED independence may be compromised.

Disclosures to be undertaken

- Annual Report disclosures of:
  - Brief terms of reference and authority of the Committee;
  - A statement of the Remuneration Policy of the company, regarding Executive Directors and NEDs;
  - Composition of the Remuneration Committee (Chairman & members);
  - Frequency of meetings;
  - Attendance of Committee members.
- Any income received by an Executive Director, who acts as a NED for another company, must be disclosed.
- Any service or employment contracts offered to directors that exceed one year.

See:

Appendix 8: Chairman of the Remuneration Committee – Job Description; and
Appendix 13: Remuneration Committee – Terms of Reference.

Score Chart

Figure 18.1 on the following page is a chart for this section of the Code.

Please refer to *Scoring Chart – ACCEPTS™ Method Instructions* (on page 53).

Following the above instructions, complete this chart first, then transcribe your results to the *Grand Score Chart* on page 197.

Excel® spreadsheet

An integrated Excel® spreadsheet model of all the individual score sheets and the *Grand Score Chart* (on page 197) is enclosed with this book.

B	BOARD REMUNERATION									Chapter 18
B.1	Remuneration - The Level & Make-Up									
	Principle: Levels of remuneration should be sufficient to attract, retain and motivate directors of the quality required to run the company successfully, but a company should avoid paying more than is necessary for this purpose. A significant proportion of executive directors' remuneration should be structured so as to link rewards to corporate and individual performance.		Date						Appendix	
	Code Provisions - Remuneration Policy									
B.1.1		**Compliance**	1	-	-	-	-	-		1 = "Yes" 0 = "No"
	The performance-related elements of remuneration should form a significant proportion of the total remuneration package of executive directors and should be designed to align their interests with those of shareholders and to give these directors keen incentives to perform at the highest levels.	**Steps Taken**								
		Compliance	1	-	-	-	-	-		1 = "Yes" 0 = "No"
	In designing schemes of performance-related remuneration, the Remuneration Committee should follow the provisions in Schedule A to this Code.	**Steps Taken**								
	Code Provisions - Remuneration Policy									
B.1.2		**Compliance**	1	-	-	-	-	-		1 = "Yes" 0 = "No"
	Executive share options should not be offered at a discount save as permitted by the relevant provisions of the Listing Rules.	**Steps Taken**								
	Code Provisions - Remuneration Policy									
B.1.3		**Compliance**	1	-	-	-	-	-		1 = "Yes" 0 = "No"
	Levels of remuneration for non-executive directors should reflect the time commitment and responsibilities of the role. Remuneration for non-executive directors should not include share options. If, exceptionally, options are granted, shareholder approval should be sought in advance and any shares acquired by exercise of the options should be held until at least one year after the non-executive director leaves the Board. Holding of share options could be relevant to the determination of a non-executive director's independence (as set out in provision A.3.1).	**Steps Taken**								

Figure 18.1

Code Provisions - Remuneration Policy											
		Compliance	1	-	-	-	-	-	-		1 = "Yes" 0 = "No"
B.1.4	Where a company releases an executive director to serve as a non-executive director elsewhere, the remuneration report should include a statement as to whether or not the director will retain such earnings and, if so, what the remuneration is.	Steps Taken									

Code Provisions - Service Contracts & Compensation											
		Compliance	1	-	-	-	-	-	-		1 = "Yes" 0 = "No"
B.1.5	The Remuneration Committee should carefully consider what compensation commitments (including pension contributions and all other elements) their directors' terms of appointment would entail in the event of early termination. The aim should be to avoid rewarding poor performance. They should take a robust line on reducing compensation to reflect departing directors' obligations to mitigate loss.	Steps Taken								13	

Code Provisions - Service Contracts & Compensation											
		Compliance	1	-	-	-	-	-	-		1 = "Yes" 0 = "No"
B.1.6	Notice or contract periods should be set at one year or less. If it isnecessary to offer longer notice or contract periods to new directors recruited from outside, such periods should reduce to one year or less after the initial period.	Steps Taken									

RESULTS

		Compliance								
The number of **complete provisions** complied with.	a	Provisions	6	.	.	.	.	.	.	-To Summary sheet
The number of **components** complied with.	b	Components	7	.	.	.	.	.	.	-To Summary sheet

		% Compliance							
Compliance rate for **complete provisions**.	a/c	Provisions	100%	.	.	.	.	.	.
Compliance rate for **components**.	b/d	Components	100%	.	.	.	.	.	.

Figure 18.1 *Continued*

Board – Rewards

(b) Procedure

What is the principle?

There should be a formal and transparent procedure for developing policy on executive remuneration and for fixing the remuneration packages of individual directors.

No director should be involved in deciding his or her own remuneration.

Supporting principles

The Remuneration Committee should consult the Chairman and/or Chief Executive about their proposals relating to the remuneration of other Executive Directors.

The Remuneration Committee should also be responsible for appointing any consultants in respect of Executive Director remuneration.

Wherever the Executive Directors or senior management are involved in advising or supporting the Remuneration Committee, care should be taken to recognize and avoid conflicts of interest.

The Chairman of the Board should ensure that the company maintains contact as required with its principal shareholders about remuneration in the same way as for other matters.

In plain English?

An objective method of setting the rewards of Executive Directors is achieved through an all-independent NED plus the CEO committee – the Remuneration Committee.

External, independent consultants should be appointed as necessary to assist the Remuneration Committee in setting the right levels of reward for each Executive Director. They may also be useful in assisting in devising an appropriate performance reward element.

The Remuneration Committee should identify its policy and members in the Annual Report. It should also have the shareholders approve the remuneration policy, together with any significant amendments as they arise.

What needs to be done?

The creation of the Remuneration Committee, with as high an independent element as can be managed, plus the CEO. This body will determine the remuneration of Executive Directors and the Chairman.

No director may take part in setting his own remuneration level.

Define a reward scheme allowing Executive Directors a means of earning significant bonuses in line with success of the company.

Declare the remuneration policy in the Annual Report and have the shareholders approve it, and any amendments to it.

The Board should set NED remuneration.

Added note

There are specific rules in *Schedule B* of the Code.

There are very specific disclosures of director's remuneration to be undertaken by quoted companies and it is not necessary to meet these demands voluntarily. None of the information sought is unavailable. It is simply a disclosure of every component of each director's package, together with the various actuarial computations, should your business be running a final salary pension scheme.

There are 7 stipulations:

1. Full details of each element of remuneration by each individual director by name. e.g. basic salary, bonuses, options, health and life insurance, pension, etc.
2. Information on share options by director by name, in accordance with ASB UITF 10.
3. If options are granted as a block, rather than phased, the report should explain and justify.
4. Pension entitlements by director by name.
5. If annual bonuses or benefits in kind are pensionable, the report should explain why.
6. 1, 2, 3 and 4 above should be subject to audit.

7. Any service contract which provide for notice periods in excess of one year should be disclosed and the reasons for longer notice periods explained.

These regulations are not considered in detail in the Code. They were the subject of extensive coverage in the Greenbury Committee Report in 1995. This ultimately became The Directors Remuneration Report Regulations 2002. Consequently, the Code expects compliance with the law and has little else to say on the matter.

Components in this section:

Code Provisions	*Reference: Appendix*	*Example/Suggestion for Compliance*
B.2.1 The Board should establish a Remuneration Committee of at least three, or in the case of smaller companies two members, who should all be independent Non-Executive Directors.	Appendix 13: Remuneration Committee – Terms of Reference	Remuneration Committee should comprise independent NEDs to the greatest extent possible. Basic and additional rewards should only be given for independently agreed performance.
The Remuneration Committee should make available its terms of reference, explaining its role and the authority delegated to it by the board.	Appendix 1: Annual Report – CG Disclosures	Remuneration Committee should outline its scope of its authority in the Annual Report.
Where remuneration consultants are appointed, a statement should be made available of whether they have any other connection with the company.		In order to determine 'market rate', a firm of Remuneration Consultants may be appointed. They should be independent, and any connections with the company should be declared.

Continued

Code Provisions	Reference: Appendix	Example/Suggestion for Compliance
B.2.2 The Remuneration Committee should have delegated responsibility for setting remuneration for all Executive Directors and the Chairman, including pension rights and any compensation payments.		The Remuneration Committee should be the exclusive body deciding the reward levels of Executive Directors and the Chairman. It should also set pension rights and compensation payments.
The committee should also recommend and monitor the level and structure of remuneration for senior management. The definition of 'senior management' for this purpose should be determined by the Board but should normally include the first layer of management below Board level.		The Remuneration Committee may extend its remit in some companies.
B.2.3 The Board itself or, where required by the Articles of Association, the shareholders should determine the remuneration of the Non-Executive Directors within the limits set in the Articles of Association.		The Board will normally set NED remuneration levels.
Where permitted by the Articles, the Board may however delegate this responsibility to a committee, which might include the Chief Executive.		

Continued

Code Provisions	*Reference: Appendix*	*Example/Suggestion for Compliance*
B.2.4 Shareholders should be invited specifically to approve all new long-term incentive schemes (as defined in the Listing Rules) and significant changes to existing schemes, save in the circumstances permitted by the Listing Rules.		The Remuneration Committee should set out its Remuneration Policy for long-term reward schemes to shareholders, who should approve it. Any significant adjustments to this policy should be referred to shareholders for further approval.

Summary checklists

Things to be created or adopted

- The Remuneration Committee.
- A significant proportion of each Executive Director's Remuneration package should become bonus-related.
- Executive Director's bonuses should be aligned to a success metric of the company.

Procedures to be created or implemented

- Annual remuneration review by the Remuneration Committee for each Executive Director and the Chairman.
- Obtain external independent information so that the Remuneration Committee can properly gauge the level of Executive Directors salary, benefits and bonus levels.
- Annual Board review of NED remuneration.
- Approve Remuneration Policy and changes at AGM.
- Chairman of the Remuneration Committee should be available at the AGM to answer any questions from shareholders.

Disclosures to be undertaken

- Remuneration Policy, together with any significant amendments.

See:

Appendix 1 – Annual Report – CG Disclosures;
Appendix 8 – Chairman of the Remuneration Committee – Job Description; and
Appendix 13 – Remuneration Committee – Terms of Reference.

Score Chart

Figure 19.1 on the following page is a chart for this section of the Code.

Please refer to Scoring Chart – ACCEPTS™ Method Instructions (on page 53).

Following the above instructions, complete this chart first, then transcribe your results to the 'Grand Score Chart' on page 197.

Excel® spreadsheet

An integrated Excel® spreadsheet model of all the individual score sheets and the 'Grand Score Chart' (on page 197) is enclosed with this book.

B	BOARD REMUNERATION	Chapter 19

B.2	Remuneration - Procedure

Principle: There should be a formal and transparent procedure for developing policy on executive remuneration and for fixing the remuneration packages of individual directors.
No director should be involved in deciding his or her own remuneration.

Code Provisions			Date							Appendix	
		Compliance	1	-	-	-	-	-	-		1 = "Yes" 0 = "No"
B.2.1	The Board should establish a Remuneration Committee of at least three, or in the case of smaller companies two, members, who should all be independent non-executive directors.	Steps Taken								13	
		Compliance	1	-	-	-	-	-	-		1 = "Yes" 0 = "No"
	The Remuneration Committee should make available its terms of reference, explaining its role and the authority delegated to it by the board.	Steps Taken									
		Compliance	1	-	-	-	-	-	-		1 = "Yes" 0 = "No"
	Where remuneration consultants are appointed, a statement should be made available of whether they have any other connection with the company.	Steps Taken									

Code Provisions											
		Compliance	1	-	-	-	-	-	-		1 = "Yes" 0 = "No"
B.2.2	The Remuneration Committee should have delegated responsibility for setting remuneration for all executive directors and the chairman, including pension rights and any compensation payments.	Steps Taken								13	
		Compliance	1	-	-	-	-	-	-		1 = "Yes" 0 = "No"
	The committee should also recommend and monitor the level and structure of remuneration for senior management. The definition of 'senior management' for this purpose should be determined by the Board but should normally include the first layer of management below Board level.	Steps Taken									

Figure 19.1

Code Provisions

B.2.3	The Board itself or, where required by the Articles of Association, the shareholders should determine the remuneration of the non-executive directors within the limits set in the Articles of Association. Where permitted by the Articles, the Board may however delegate this responsibility to a committee, which might include the chief executive.	**Compliance**	1	-	-	-	-	-	-		1 = "Yes" 0 = "No"
		Steps Taken									

Code Provisions

B.2.4	Shareholders should be invited specifically to approve all new long-term incentive schemes (as defined in the Listing Rules) and significant changes to existing schemes, save in the circumstances permitted by the Listing Rules.	**Compliance**	1	-	-	-	-	-	-		1 = "Yes" 0 = "No"
		Steps Taken									

RESULTS

		Compliance								
The number of **complete provisions** complied with.	a	Provisions	4	.	.	.	.	.	.	-To Summary sheet
The number of **components** complied with.	b	Components	7	.	.	.	.	.	.	-To Summary sheet

		% Compliance							
Compliance rate for **complete provisions**.	a/c	Provisions	100%	.	.	.	.	.	.
Compliance rate for **components**.	b/d	Components	100%	.	.	.	.	.	.

Figure 19.1 *Continued*

SCHEDULE A: PROVISIONS ON THE DESIGN OF PERFORMANCE RELATED REMUNERATION

1. The Remuneration Committee should consider whether the directors should be eligible for annual bonuses. If so, performance conditions should be relevant, stretching and designed to enhance shareholder value.
   Upper limits should be set and disclosed. There may be a case for part payment in shares to be held for a significant period.

2. The Remuneration Committee should consider whether the directors should be eligible for benefits under long-term incentive schemes.
   Traditional share option schemes should be weighed against other kinds of long-term incentive scheme.
   In normal circumstances, shares granted or other forms of deferred remuneration should not vest, and options should not be exercisable, in less than three years.
   Directors should be encouraged to hold their shares for a further period after vesting or exercise, subject to the need to finance any costs of acquisition and associated tax liabilities.

3. Any new long-term incentive schemes which are proposed should be approved by shareholders and should preferably replace any existing schemes or at least form part of a well considered overall plan, incorporating existing schemes. The total rewards potentially available should not be excessive.

4. Payouts or grants under all incentive schemes, including new grants under existing share option schemes, should be subject to challenging performance criteria reflecting the company's objectives. Consideration should be given to criteria which reflect the company's performance relative to a group of comparator companies in some key variables such as total shareholder return.

5. Grants under executive share option and other long-term incentive schemes should normally be phased rather than awarded in one large block.

6. In general, only basic salary should be pensionable.

7. The Remuneration Committee should consider the pension consequences and associated costs to the company of basic salary increases and any other changes in pensionable remuneration, especially for directors close to retirement.

SCHEDULE B: PROVISIONS ON WHAT SHOULD BE INCLUDED IN THE REMUNERATION REPORT

1. Full details of each element of remuneration by each individual director by name. Eg basic salary, bonuses, options, health and life insurance, pension, etc.

2. Information on share options by director by name, in accordance with ASB UITF 10.

3. If options are granted as a block, rather than phased, the report should explain and justify.

4. Pension entitlements by director by name.

5. If annual bonuses or benefits in kind are pensionable, the report should explain why.

6. 1, 2, 3 and 4 above should be subject to audit.

7. Any service contract which provide for notice periods in excess of one year should be disclosed and the reasons for the longer notice periods explained.

Figure 19.1 *Continued*

Accountability

(a) Financial Reporting

What is the principle?

The Board should present a balanced and understandable assessment of the company's position and prospects.

Supporting principle

The Board's responsibility to present a balanced and understandable assessment extends to interim and other price-sensitive public reports and reports to regulators as well as to information required to be presented by statutory requirements.

In plain English?

The Board is responsible for the production of the financial statements contained in the Annual Report. The financial statements are the Profit and Loss account, the Balance Sheet, the Funds Flow statement and all the associated notes to these.

The auditors are responsible for reporting that the financial statements show a true and fair view of the company's performance and position. They demonstrate this through the Audit Report.

The detection of fraud is not the auditor's primary concern. They can however, detect fraud and should report if it is found.

The Board should ensure that the financial statements are clear and meaningful. It should also ensure that they are representative of the company's performance and position. This means the avoidance of racy or overly optimistic assumptions and, equally, overly-pessimistic assumptions.

If the Board regards the company as a 'going concern', it should say so. This means the Board is confident the company will still be in business in the medium term. Being wrong on this point is only an offence if the statement is made recklessly or falsely.

What needs to be done?

An explanation of the responsibilities of both the Board and the auditors should be made in the Annual Report. (It is probably there already, at the auditor's suggestion.)

The Board should be satisfied that the company is a 'going concern'.

This statement should be based on the company's projections, budgets and cash flow forecasts.

Therefore, the company must produce trading projections, budgets and cash flow forecasts to the Board so that the 'going concern' status can be judged sensibly with good supporting information. Any qualifications to the 'going concern' statement must be detailed in the Annual Report.

Components in this section:

Code Provisions	*Reference: Appendix*	*Example/Suggestion for Compliance*
C.1.1 The directors should explain in the Annual Report their responsibility for preparing the accounts and there should be a statement by the auditors about their reporting responsibilities.	Appendix 1: Annual Report – CG Disclosures	The Annual Report preparation is the responsibility of the Board, and should say so. The auditors should also state their responsibilities in the Annual Report.
C.1.2 The directors should report that the business is a going concern, with supporting assumptions or qualifications as necessary.	Appendix 1: Annual Report – CG Disclosures	A statement that the company is a 'going concern' should be included in the Annual Report. The value of the company is highly compromised if it is not a 'going concern'. If the statement of 'going concern' can only be made conditionally, those conditions should be explained in the Annual Report.

Summary checklists

Things to be created or adopted

- The Audit Committee with at least two NEDs, one of whom should be financially literate and experienced (see *Chapter 22*).
- The Terms of Reference of the Audit Committee.
- A Chairman of the Audit Committee.
- Create a sensible and legal definition of what the company being a 'going concern' actually means. This could be cash, sales and/or profit performance over the next 18 months, for example. If in any doubt, discuss this with your auditors. They will be working with your own definition, whether you realize it or not!

Procedures to be created or implemented

- (At least) Annual review of budgets and cash flow forecasts by the Board to specifically support the statement that the business is a 'going concern'.
- Regardless of who produces them, the Board (through the Audit Committee) should review the financial statements and acknowledge responsibility for them.
- Chairman of the Audit Committee should be available at the AGM to answer any questions from shareholders.

Disclosures to be undertaken

- Annual Report disclosures of:
  - Brief terms of reference and authority of the Committee;
  - Composition of the Audit Committee and qualifications (Chairman & members);
  - Frequency of meetings;
  - Attendance of Committee members.
- A description of main activities:
  - Monitoring the integrity of the Financial Statements;
  - Review of Internal Control and Risk Management systems;
  - Review of external auditor independence.

- Statement of Board responsibility for the production of the financial statements contained in the Annual Report.
- Statement of Auditor responsibility for producing their opinion of the financial statements contained in the Annual Report.
- Statement by the Board that the company is a 'going concern', together with qualifying assumptions (if any), in the Annual Report.

See:

Chapter 22: Accountability (c) Audit Committee & Auditors;
Appendix 1: Annual Report – CG Disclosures;
Appendix 9: Chairman of the Audit Committee – Job Description; and
Appendix 14: Audit Committee – Terms of Reference.

Score Chart

Figure 20.1 on the following page is a chart for this section of the Code.

Please refer to *Scoring Chart – ACCEPTS™ Method Instructions* (on page 53).

Following the above instructions, complete this chart first, then transcribe your results to the *Grand Score Chart* on page 197.

Excel® spreadsheet

An integrated Excel® spreadsheet model of all the individual score sheets and the *Grand Score Chart* (on page 197) is enclosed with this book.

C	ACCOUNTABILITY & AUDIT	Chapter 20

C.1	Financial Reporting

Principle:

The Board should present a balanced and understandable assessment of the company's position and prospects.

			Date						Appendix
Code Provisions									
		Compliance	1	-	-	-	-	-	1 = "Yes" 0 = "No"
C.1.1	The directors should explain in the Annual Report their responsibility for preparing the accounts and there should be a statement by the auditors about their reporting responsibilities.	**Steps Taken**							1
Code Provisions									
		Compliance	1	-	-	-	-	-	1 = "Yes" 0 = "No"
C.1.2	The directors should report that the business is a going concern, with supporting assumptions or qualifications as necessary.	**Steps Taken**							1

RESULTS

		Compliance							
The number of **complete provisions** complied with.	a	Provisions	2	.	.	.	.	.	-To Summary sheet
The number of **components** complied with.	b	Components	2	.	.	.	.	.	-To Summary sheet

		% Compliance						
Compliance rate for **complete provisions**.	a/c	Provisions	100%	.	.	.	.	.
Compliance rate for **components**.	b/d	Components	100%	.	.	.	.	.

Figure 20.1

Accountability

(b) Internal Control

What is the principle?

The Board should maintain a sound system of internal control to safeguard the shareholders' investment and the company's assets.

In plain English?

The Board is responsible for safeguarding the shareholders' investment and the company's assets.

There was a time when a sound system of internal control simply meant the financial controls, such as the signature processes for authorizing cheques and the physical protection of stocks and finished goods.

The Code now squarely makes the Board responsible for *all* risks to the shareholders' investment and the company's assets, financial or otherwise.

For example, Board responsibility now encompasses contractual risk, compliance risk (employment, pollution, health & safety, etc.), as well as commercial and business risk.

What needs to be done?

The regular internal controls, that regulate cheque payments, authorization of invoices, stock control, management structure, etc. are assumed to be in place as a minimum.

Your business is also exposed to other types of risk that may cause loss, not just financial.

Other areas of risk include operational and compliance risk. Operational risks might include reputational damage caused by a design fault in a new product. Compliance risk might include falling foul of new waste control regulations, where the company remains unaware and is heavily fined for environmental damage.

The Board should establish proper Risk Management practices, including Business Continuity Planning. Your insurers may already be asking for this to be done.

The Board should be able to state:

- It maintains full control and direction over appropriate strategic, financial, organizational and compliance issues;

- It has put in place an organizational structure with formally defined lines of responsibility and delegation of authority;
- It has delegated to the senior management team the implementation of the systems of internal financial control within an established framework that applies throughout the company;
- That an internal control framework can only provide reasonable, although not absolute, assurance against material misstatement or loss; and
- The directors are not aware of any significant weakness or deficiencies in the company's system of internal control.

Components in this section:

Code Provisions	*Reference: Appendix*	*Example/Suggestion for Compliance*
C.2.1 The Board should, at least annually, conduct a review of the effectiveness of the group's system of internal controls and should report to shareholders that they have done so.	Appendix 1: Annual Report – CG Disclosures	The Board is obliged to examine how effective the company's internal controls are each year. These are controls that safeguard the company's assets (against fraud or misuse) and protect the shareholders' investment. A statement that this has been done should be made in the Annual Report.
The review should cover all material controls, including financial, operational and compliance controls and risk management systems.		The review should not be confined to financial controls, but should also include all other controls – including risk assessment.

Summary checklists

Things to be created or adopted

- The Audit Committee.

Procedures to be created or implemented

- Risk assessment procedures.
- Business continuity and disaster recovery planning.

Disclosures to be undertaken

- An assurance regarding internal controls and risk assessment in the Annual Report.

See:

Appendix 1: Annual Report – CG Disclosures.

Score Chart

Figure 21.1 on the following page is a chart for this section of the Code.

Please refer to *Scoring Chart – ACCEPTS™ Method Instructions* (on page 53).

Following the above instructions, complete this chart first, then transcribe your results to the *Grand Score Chart* on page 197.

Excel® spreadsheet

An integrated Excel® spreadsheet model of all the individual score sheets and the *Grand Score Chart* (on page 197) is enclosed with this book.

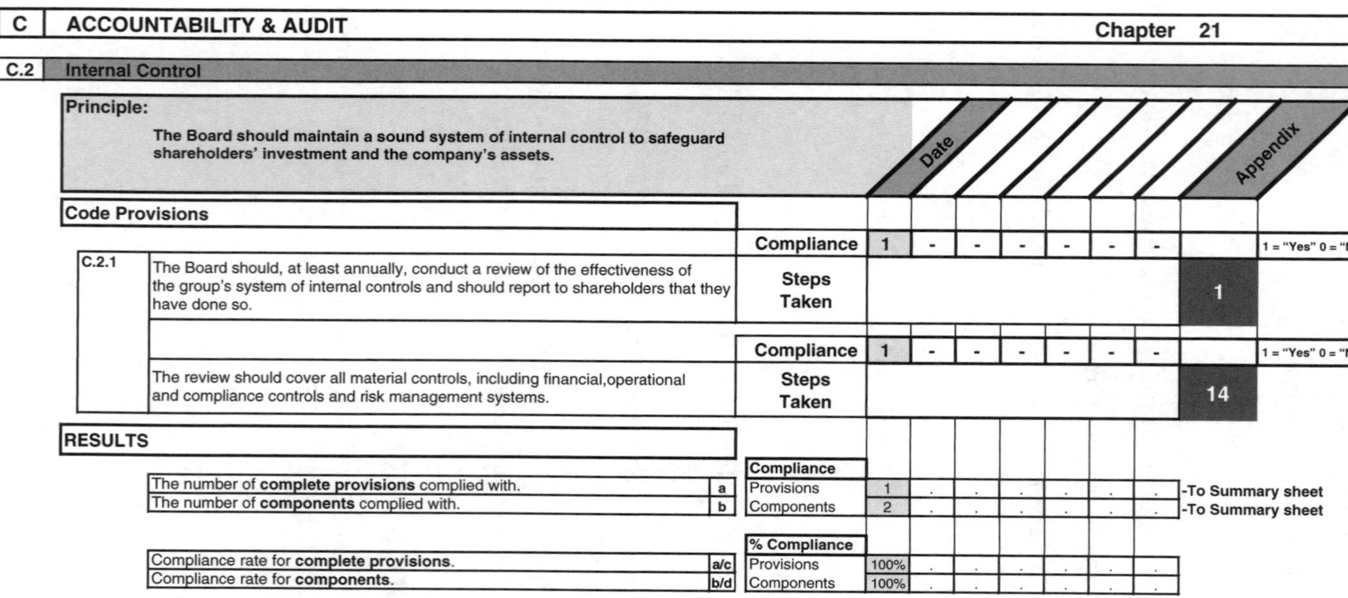
C ACCOUNTABILITY & AUDIT
Chapter 21
C.2 Internal Control
Principle:
The Board should maintain a sound system of internal control to safeguard shareholders' investment and the company's assets.
Date
Appendix
Code Provisions
Compliance 1 - - - - - -
1 = "Yes" 0 = "No"
C.2.1
The Board should, at least annually, conduct a review of the effectiveness of the group's system of internal controls and should report to shareholders that they have done so.
Steps Taken
1
Compliance 1 - - - - - -
1 = "Yes" 0 = "No"
The review should cover all material controls, including financial,operational and compliance controls and risk management systems.
Steps Taken
14
RESULTS
The number of complete provisions complied with. a
The number of components complied with. b
Compliance
Provisions 1
Components 2
-To Summary sheet
-To Summary sheet
Compliance rate for complete provisions. a/c
Compliance rate for components. b/d
% Compliance
Provisions 100%
Components 100%

Figure 21.1

22 Accountability

(c) Audit Committee and Auditors

What is the principle?

The Board should establish formal and transparent arrangements for considering how they should apply the financial reporting and internal control principles, and for maintaining an appropriate relationship with the company's external auditors.

In plain English?

The 'formal and transparent' arrangements refer to the establishment of an Audit Committee.

It is this committee that will review the financial statements in the Annual Report for clarity and accuracy.

'Clarity' means that they are as easy as possible to understand.

'Accuracy' refers to the consistent application of accounting policies and the avoidance of unlikely assumptions.

This committee will also review the suitability of the internal control systems and the general risk management systems of the company.

The independence of the external auditors will also be reviewed and this committee will be the main liaison with them.

The Audit Committee also brings together the functions of internal auditor (if any) and external audit.

Finding suitable NEDs to sit on the Audit Committee can be problematic, due to the skill and experience requirements, mentioned above.

What needs to be done?

Set up an Audit Committee comprising at least three independent NEDs, one of whom should be financially literate and experienced (Two independent NEDs in smaller companies).

Set out a list of responsibilities for approval by the Board. These are well laid out in the ICSA guidelines (Appendix 14: Audit Committee – Terms of Reference) and include:

- Monitoring the integrity of all financial information announced externally, including the Annual Report;

- Reviewing the performance of internal control systems;
- Reviewing the effectiveness of Risk Management systems (a separate Board committee may be set up to deal with this, specifically);
- Review the work of the internal audit function, if any;
- If not, annually review the need for an internal audit function and state reasons why not in the Annual Report;
- Recommend the selection, appointment and removal of external auditors to the shareholders at AGM;
- Review the engagement terms and remuneration of the external auditors;
- Monitor the level of non-audit work performed by the auditors and the implications for independence;
- Remain current on UK regulations regarding auditor independence; and
- Establish a 'Whistle-blowing' Procedure for staff to follow when wrongdoing is suspected and, in particular, when line managers may not be available to resolve – as they may be involved.

The policy and activities of the Audit Committee should be disclosed in the Annual Report, together with the names of the committee members and the number of times they met.

The Audit Committee should ensure that the Annual Report also states:

- If the external auditors provide non-audit services, outline what these services are and state how their independence and objectivity is safeguarded;
- That there is an effective internal audit function (if any); or
- That the committee has reviewed the need for an internal audit function and has concluded it is not necessary because — (state reason);
- That a Whistle-blower Procedure exists (if it does).

Finally, the AGM resolutions regarding appointment or re-appointment of auditors and their remuneration should be supplied under the authority of the Audit Committee.

Components in this section:

Code Provisions	*Reference: Appendix*	*Example/Suggestion for Compliance*
C.3.1 The Board should establish an Audit Committee of at least three, or in the case of smaller companies two members, who should all be independent Non-Executive Directors.	Appendix 14: Audit Committee – Terms of Reference	An Audit Committee should be set up. There should be three independent NEDs. (Smaller companies – two independent NEDs).
The Board should satisfy itself that at least one member of the Audit Committee has recent and relevant financial experience.		At least one of the independent NEDs on the committee should be financially literate and experienced.
C.3.2 The main role and responsibilities of the Audit Committee should be set out in written terms of reference and should include:	Appendix 14: Audit Committee – Terms of Reference	Set up the Audit Committee with a list of formal responsibilities, sanctioned by the Board.
– to monitor the integrity of the financial statements of the company, and any formal announcements relating to the company's financial performance, reviewing significant financial reporting judgements contained in them;		The Audit Committee must monitor all financial information announced externally – not just the Annual Report.
– to review the company's internal	Appendix 14: Audit	The Audit Committee should review the

Continued

Code Provisions		Reference: Appendix	Example/Suggestion for Compliance
C.3.2 (contd.)	financial controls and, unless expressly addressed by a separate Board risk committee composed of independent directors, or by the Board itself, to review the company's internal control and risk management systems;	Committee – Terms of Reference	performance of internal controls. Unless a separate Risk Committee is set up, the Audit Committee should review the company's Risk Management systems.
	– to monitor and review the effectiveness of the company's internal audit function;		Where there is one, the Audit Committee should review the company's internal audit function.
	– to make recommendations to the Board, for it to put to the shareholders for their approval in general meeting, in relation to the appointment, re-appointment and removal of the external auditor and to approve the remuneration and terms of engagement of the external auditor;		The Audit Committee should select, appoint and remove the external auditors, via the AGM. The auditor's terms of engagement and remuneration should also be approved by this committee.
	– to review and monitor the external auditor's independence and objectivity and the effectiveness of the audit process, taking into consideration relevant UK professional and regulatory requirements;		The Audit Committee should apply the independence criteria to the external auditors, while keeping abreast of UK regulations on this requirement.

Continued

Code Provisions		Reference: Appendix	Example/Suggestion for Compliance
C.3.2 (contd.)	– to develop and implement policy on the engagement of the external auditor to supply non-audit services, taking into account relevant ethical guidance regarding the provision of non-audit services by the external audit firm; and to report to the Board, identifying any matters in respect of which it considers that action or improvement is needed and making recommendations as to the steps to be taken.		The Audit Committee should review how much non-audit work is done by the external auditors, recommending any actions the Board should take to avoid conflicts of interests.
C.3.3	The terms of reference of the Audit Committee, including its role and the authority delegated to it by the Board, should be made available. A separate section of the Annual Report should describe the work of the committee in discharging those responsibilities.	Appendix 14: Audit Committee – Terms of Reference	Audit Committee duties should be authorized by the Board in line with the ICSA guidelines.
		Appendix 1: Annual Report – CG Disclosures	These duties and responsibilities should be summarized in the Annual Report.
C.3.4	The Audit Committee should review arrangements by which staff of the company may, in confidence, raise concerns about possible improprieties in matters of financial reporting or other matters.	Appendix 14: Audit Committee – Terms of Reference	A conduit should be established to allow staff to raise concerns without following the normal line-management structure.
		Appendix 11: The Whistle-blowing Procedure	A Whistle-blowing Procedure should be put in place.

Continued

Code Provisions		Reference: Appendix	Example/Suggestion for Compliance
C.3.4 (contd.)	The Audit Committee's objective should be to ensure that arrangements are in place for the proportionate and independent investigation of such matters and for appropriate follow-up action.		
C.3.5	The Audit Committee should monitor and review the effectiveness of the internal audit activities.	Appendix 14: Audit Committee – Terms of Reference	The Audit Committee should involve itself in the internal audit function, reviewing its activities, findings and effectiveness.
	Where there is no internal audit function, the Audit Committee should consider annually whether there is a need for an internal audit function and make a recommendation to the Board, and the reasons for the absence of such a function should be explained in the relevant section of the Annual Report.	Appendix 1: Annual Report – CG Disclosures	Where there isn't one, the Audit Committee should annually review if the company needs an internal audit function. If felt unnecessary, the reasons should be explained in the Annual Report.
C.3.6	The Audit Committee should have primary responsibility for making a recommendation on the appointment, reappointment and removal of the external auditors. If the Board does not accept the Audit Committee's		The Audit Committee should choose the company's auditors. If the Audit Committee selection of auditor is not accepted by the Board, an explanation should be given in the Annual Report regarding the Board's differing view

Continued

Code Provisions		*Reference: Appendix*	*Example/Suggestion for Compliance*
C.3.6 (contd.)	recommendation, it should include in the Annual Report, and in any papers recommending appointment or re-appointment, a statement from the Audit Committee explaining the recommendation and should set out reasons why the Board has taken a different position.		
C.3.7	The Annual Report should explain to shareholders how, if the auditor provides non-audit services, auditor objectivity and independence is safeguarded.	Appendix 1: Annual Report – CG Disclosures	This is a deterrent to giving large quantities of non-audit work to the auditors. It is common for the auditors of smaller companies to perform tax computations and submissions. Even this may be outlawed in the future. The statement of 'independence being safeguarded' must be honestly included in the Annual Report.

Summary checklists

Things to be created or adopted

- The Audit Committee, comprising at least 3 independent NEDs (2 in smaller companies) with at least one experienced in finance.
- Board authority and Terms of Reference.
- Audit Committee to form a Whistle-blowing Procedure.

Procedures to be created or implemented

- Audit Committee to review the clarity and integrity of all external financial disclosures, including the Annual Report.
- Audit Committee to review the adequacy of Internal Control systems.
- Audit Committee to review adequacy of Risk Management systems (if not already done by a separate committee).
- Audit Committee to review the work and effectiveness of the Internal Audit function (if any).
- Audit Committee to recommend appointment/re-appointment/remuneration of external auditors, recommending AGM resolutions for these to the Board.
- Audit Committee to monitor the level of non-audit work done by the external auditors and form an opinion regarding their ongoing independence.

Disclosures to be undertaken

- Details of the Audit Committee in the Annual Report – its policy, authority, membership, function and frequency of meeting.
- An explanation, if needed, as to the type and quantity of non-audit work undertaken by the external auditors, and how their independence is being protected.
- An explanation, if needed, as to why there is no requirement for an Internal Audit function.
- An explanation, if needed, as to why the external auditors recommended for selection by the Audit Committee differed from the selection of the Board.
- That a Whistle-blower Procedure exists.

See:

Appendix 1: Annual Report – CG Disclosures;
Appendix 9: Chairman of the Audit Committee – Job Description;
Appendix 11: The Whistle-blowing Procedure; and
Appendix 14: Audit Committee – Terms of Reference.

Score Chart

Figure 22.1 on the following page is a chart for this section of the Code.

Please refer to *Scoring Chart – ACCEPTS™ Method Instructions* (on page 53).

Following the above instructions, complete this chart first, then transcribe your results to the *Grand Score Chart* on page 197.

Excel® spreadsheet

An integrated Excel® spreadsheet model of all the individual score sheets and the *Grand Score Chart* (on page 197) is enclosed with this book.

C	ACCOUNTABILITY & AUDIT		Chapter 22								
C.3	Audit Committee & Auditors										
	Principle: **The Board should establish formal and transparent arrangements for considering how they should apply the financial reporting and internal control principles, and for maintaining an appropriate relationship with the company's external auditors.**		Date							Appendix	
	Code Provisions										
C.3.1		**Compliance**	1	-	-	-	-	-	-		1 = "Yes" 0 = "No"
	The Board should establish an Audit Committee of at least three, or in the case of smaller companies two, members, who should all be independent non-executive directors.	**Steps Taken**								14	
		Compliance	1	-	-	-	-	-	-		1 = "Yes" 0 = "No"
	The Board should satisfy itself that at least one member of the Audit Committee has recent and relevant financial experience.	**Steps Taken**									
	Code Provisions										
C.3.2		**Compliance**	1	-	-	-	-	-	-		1 = "Yes" 0 = "No"
	The main role and responsibilities of the Audit Committee should be set out in written terms of reference and should include:	**Steps Taken**								14	
		Compliance	1	-	-	-	-	-	-		1 = "Yes" 0 = "No"
	- to monitor the integrity of the financial statements of the company, and any formal announcements relating to the company's financial performance, reviewing significant financial reporting judgements contained in them;	**Steps Taken**									
		Compliance	1	-	-	-	-	-	-		1 = "Yes" 0 = "No"
	- to review the company's internal financial controls and, unless expressly addressed by a separate Board risk committee composed of independent directors, or by the Board itself, to review the company's internal control and risk management systems;	**Steps Taken**								9	

Figure 22.1

		Compliance	1	-	-	-	-	-	-		1 = "Yes" 0 = "No"
	- to monitor and review the effectiveness of the company's internal audit function;	Steps Taken									
		Compliance	1	-	-	-	-	-	-		1 = "Yes" 0 = "No"
	- to make recommendations to the Board, for it to put to the shareholders for their approval in general meeting, in relation to the appointment, re-appointment and removal of the external auditor and to approve the remuneration and terms of engagement of the external auditor;	Steps Taken									
		Compliance	1	-	-	-	-	-	-		1 = "Yes" 0 = "No"
	- to review and monitor the external auditor's independence and objectivity and the effectiveness of the audit process, taking into consideration relevant UK professional and regulatory requirements;	Steps Taken									
		Compliance	1	-	-	-	-	-	-		1 = "Yes" 0 = "No"
	- to develop and implement policy on the engagement of the external auditor to supply non-audit services, taking into account relevant ethical guidance regarding the provision of non-audit services by the external audit firm; and to report to the Board, identifying any matters in respect of which it considers that action or improvement is needed and making recommendations as to the steps to be taken.	Steps Taken									
Code Provisions											
		Compliance	1	-	-	-	-	-	-		1 = "Yes" 0 = "No"
C.3.3	The terms of reference of the Audit Committee, including its role and the authority delegated to it by the Board, should be made available. A separate section of the Annual Report should describe the work of the committee in discharging those responsibilities.	Steps Taken								14	

Figure 22.1 *Continued*

Code Provisions											
		Compliance	1	-	-	-	-	-			1 = "Yes" 0 = "No"
C.3.4	The Audit Committee should review arrangements by which staff of thecompany may, in confidence, raise concerns about possible improprieties in matters of financial reporting or other matters. The Audit Committee's objective should be to ensure that arrangements are in place for the proportionate and independent investigation of such matters and for appropriate follow-up action.	Steps Taken								11	

Code Provisions											
		Compliance	1	-	-	-	-	-			1 = "Yes" 0 = "No"
C.3.5	The Audit Committee should monitor and review the effectiveness of the internal audit activities.	Steps Taken								14	
		Compliance	1	-	-	-	-	-			1 = "Yes" 0 = "No"
	Where there is no internal audit function, the Audit Committee should consider annually whether there is a need for an internal audit function and make a recommendation to the Board, and the reasons for the absence of such a function should be explained in the relevant section of the Annual Report.	Steps Taken									

Code Provisions											
		Compliance	1	-	-	-	-	-			1 = "Yes" 0 = "No"
C.3.6	The Audit Committee should have primary responsibility for making a recommendation on the appointment, reappointment and removal of the external auditors. If the Board does not accept the Audit Committee's recommendation, it should include in the Annual Report, and in any papers recommending appointment or re-appointment, a statement from the Audit Committee explaining the recommendation and should set out reasons why the Board has taken a different position.	Steps Taken								14	

Figure 22.1 *Continued*

Code Provisions

		Compliance	1	-	-	-	-	-	-		1 = "Yes" 0 = "No"
C.3.7	The Annual Report should explain to shareholders how, if the auditor provides non-audit services, auditor objectivity and independence is safeguarded.	**Steps Taken**								1	

RESULTS

		Compliance								
The number of **complete provisions** complied with.	a	Provisions	7	.	.	.	.	.	.	-To Summary sheet
The number of **components** complied with.	b	Components	15	.	.	.	.	.	.	-To Summary sheet

		% Compliance							
Compliance rate for **complete provisions**.	a/c	Provisions	100%	.	.	.	.	.	.
Compliance rate for **components**.	b/d	Components	100%	.	.	.	.	.	.

Figure 22.1 *Continued*

Relations with Shareholders – Dialogue

What is the principle?

There should be a dialogue with shareholders based on the mutual understanding of objectives. The Board as a whole has responsibility for ensuring that a satisfactory dialogue with shareholders takes place.

Supporting principles

Whilst recognizing that most shareholder contact is with the Chief Executive and finance director, the Chairman (and the senior independent director and other directors as appropriate) should maintain sufficient contact with major shareholders to understand their issues and concerns.

The Board should keep in touch with shareholder opinion in whatever ways are most practical and efficient.

In plain English?

The Board has an obligation to understand the requirements of the company's shareholders. The Board has more chance of pleasing them if it knows what they want. This may seem obvious – it is!

In the preceding chapters, we have seen how the Code mercilessly pursues objectivity, independence, accountability and openness. All shareholders will have a common appreciation of these things and they can be applied without any knowledge at all of the characteristics of the shareholders or the business itself.

However, there are certain aspects of the Code where knowledge of the shareholders does matter.

Against what measure, for example, does the Board decide an appropriate level of risk? How do you build risk management systems without knowing what is 'normal risk'?

A property development company and a sheltered housing association will have differing levels of acceptable risk in the projects they undertake.

An oil prospecting company will accept very high risks in its business in comparison to a florist.

These are subjective criteria. The Board has no way of knowing what is an acceptable 'normal' level of risk to shareholders without understanding the risk profile of the major shareholders.

There is no way of understanding the risk profile of the major shareholders without meeting them. Not only should the Chairman meet shareholders, but also the other NEDs, too. This will ensure that the various committees applying the CG principles will have better knowledge of what the shareholders expect.

What needs to be done?

The Chairman and NEDs, particularly the Senior NED, should meet with major shareholders. They should discuss strategy and CG matters. The NEDs should make themselves aware of their expectations and aspirations, also listening to any concerns they may have. Formulating an opinion of acceptable risk is a critical outcome of this dialogue.

The Annual Report should make reference to steps taken to develop and improve the dialogue between Board and shareholders. This is a fairly simple task for the unquoted company to undertake. An unquoted company will not have a diversity of institutional shareholders (e.g. pension and insurance funds) to maintain dialogue with, or an army of private investors. There is a separate section of the Code specifically aimed at the institutional shareholders and how they should deal with quoted companies (Section E). This is the converse of what is being discussed here and is not relevant to the aspiring SME. It is not dealt with in this book.

Unquoted companies may have venture capital investors, the nearest equivalent to an institutional investor. However, they are usually represented on the Board and have an intimate knowledge of the company already.

Unquoted companies may also have a myriad of share incentive schemes, thus creating an army of shareholders through the workforce. Dialogue with this (already informed) group is not usually difficult. Therefore, compliance with this section is relatively straightforward.

Components in this section:

Code Provisions	Reference: Appendix	Example/Suggestion for Compliance
D.1.1 The Chairman should ensure that the views of shareholders are communicated to the Board as a whole. The Chairman should discuss governance and strategy with major shareholders. Non-Executive Directors should be offered the opportunity to attend meetings with major shareholders and should expect to attend them if requested by major shareholders. The senior independent director should attend sufficient meetings with a range of major shareholders to listen to their views in order to help develop a balanced understanding of the issues and concerns of major shareholders.		The Chairman bridges a link between the Board and the major shareholders. CG should be discussed with the shareholders. NEDs should also meet with the shareholders to develop an understanding of what represents their major issues, and what causes them concern. This understanding clarifies qualitative, subjective aspects of the shareholder profile. For example, it is not possible to quantify the comfortable ambient level of risk that is acceptable to the shareholders without meeting a representative cross section.
D.1.2 The Board should state in the Annual Report the steps they have taken to ensure that the members of the Board, and in particular the Non-Executive Directors, develop an understanding of the views of major shareholders about their company, for example through direct face-to-face contact, analysts' or brokers' briefings and surveys of shareholder opinion.	Appendix 1: Annual Report – CG Disclosures	In the Annual Report, the Board should outline the steps it has taken to develop and improve its understanding of the views of shareholders.

Summary checklists

Things to be created or adopted

- None.

Procedures to be created or implemented

- Regular meetings of the Chairman, Senior NED (and other NEDs as available) with major shareholders.
- Discussions amongst the NEDs and, subsequently, the Board regarding expectations and concerns of the shareholders.

Disclosures to be undertaken

- The steps taken to improve and develop dialogue with the shareholders can usefully be outlined in the Annual Report.

See:

Appendix 1: Annual Report – CG Disclosures.

Score Chart

Figure 23.1 on the following page is a chart for this section of the Code.

Please refer to *Scoring Chart – ACCEPTS™ Method Instructions* (on page 53).

Following the above instructions, complete this chart first, then transcribe your results to the *Grand Score Chart* on page 197.

Excel® spreadsheet

An integrated Excel® spreadsheet model of all the individual score sheets and the *Grand Score Chart* (on page 197) is enclosed with this book.

D	RELATIONS WITH SHAREHOLDERS	Chapter 23

D.1	Dialogue With Institutional Shareholders

Principle:
There should be a dialogue with shareholders based on the mutual understanding of objectives. The Board as a whole has responsibility for ensuring that a satisfactory dialogue with shareholders takes place.

Code Provisions			Date							Appendix	
		Compliance	1	-	-	-	-	-	-		1 = "Yes" 0 = "No"
D.1.1	The chairman should ensure that the views of shareholders are communicated to the Board as a whole. The chairman should discuss governance and strategy with major shareholders. Non-executive directors should be offered the opportunity to attend meetings with major shareholders and should expect to attend them if requested by major shareholders. The senior independent director should attend sufficient meetings with a range of major shareholders to listen to their views in order to help develop a balanced understanding of the issues and concerns of major shareholders.	Steps Taken									

Code Provisions											
		Compliance	1	-	-	-	-	-	-		1 = "Yes" 0 = "No"
D.1.2	The Board should state in the Annual Report the steps they have taken to ensure that the members of the Board, and in particular the non-executive directors, develop an understanding of the views of major shareholders about their company, for example through direct face-to-face contact, analysts' or brokers' briefings and surveys of shareholder opinion.	Steps Taken								1	

Figure 23.1

RESULTS

		Compliance								
The number of **complete provisions** complied with.	**a**	Provisions	2	.	.	.	.	.	.	-To Summary sheet
The number of **components** complied with.	**b**	Components	2	.	.	.	.	.	.	-To Summary sheet
		% Compliance								
Compliance rate for **complete provisions.**	**a/c**	Provisions	100%	.	.	.	.	.	.	
Compliance rate for **components.**	**b/d**	Components	100%	.	.	.	.	.	.	

Figure 23.1 *Continued*

Relations with Shareholders – Constructive Use of the AGM

What is the principle?

The Board should use the Annual General Meeting (AGM) to communicate with investors and to encourage their participation.

Supporting principles

None.

In plain English?

The AGM is a meeting of the shareholders and the Board.

The Board accounts to the shareholders for its stewardship of the company's assets. This creates an opportunity to communicate the company's objectives, broad strategy and future prospects, which should be sympathetic to the requirements of the majority of shareholders.

For example, the Board should be aware of the risk profile that is acceptable to the shareholders and create strategies on that basis.

Ultimately, an informed shareholder should be more willing to participate in the affairs of the company, including the AGM. It is desirable to have this loop of communication and shareholder feedback that is facilitated by the AGM.

What needs to be done?

Extend the notice period for the AGM from the statutory 14 days to a minimum of 20 working days. This provides shareholders with a greater opportunity to attend.

At the AGM itself, the Nomination, Remuneration and Audit Committee Chairman should attend so that all questions of CG and CG policy can be answered.

All resolutions should be distinct and map individually to each issue. They should not be aggregated together.

A resolution should always be put to the AGM regarding the adoption of the Annual Report and accounts.[1]

After a 'show of hands' vote has been resolved, the Chairman should announce the total proxies that had been received both 'for' and 'against' the resolution.

Components in this section:

Code Provisions	*Reference: Appendix*	*Example/Suggestion for Compliance*
D.2.1 The company should count all proxy votes and, except where a poll is called, should indicate the level of proxies lodged on each resolution, and the balance for and against the resolution and the number of abstentions, after it has been dealt with on a show of hands. The company should ensure that votes cast are properly received and recorded.		When the result of the vote on a resolution is announced by the Chairman after a show of hands, he should also indicate the number of proxy votes cast on that resolution. All votes cast should be properly recorded and the company should be rigorous in getting this right.
D.2.2 The company should propose a separate resolution at the AGM on each substantially separate issue and should in particular		The company should propose a resolution on the adoption of the Annual Report & accounts.

[1] This is a vote of approval, as would be a vote on the company's remuneration policy. Consider if the shareholders voted against the adoption of the accounts.
What does that actually mean? What it *cannot* mean is 'take the accounts away, do them again – producing a different result – and have somebody else audit them'!
The accounts have been prepared and audited under the Companies Acts 1985 & 1989, as well as in accordance with the prevailing audit standards.
Shareholders can only exhibit displeasure with the picture being portrayed in the financial statements and, of course, the performance of the directors.

Code Provisions	*Reference Appendix*	*Example/Suggestion for Compliance*
D.2.2 (contd.) propose a resolution at the AGM relating to the report and accounts.		Separate, clear, individual resolutions should be proposed at the AGM for each substantive issue.
D.2.3 The Chairman should arrange for the chairmen of the Audit, Remuneration and Nomination Committees to be available to answer questions at the AGM and for all directors to attend.		Attendance of all the committee chairmen should mean that all questions of CG and CG policy can be answered.
D.2.4 The company should arrange for the notice of the AGM and related papers to be sent to shareholders at least 20 working days before the meeting.		Allow 20 working days of notice before the AGM instead of the statutory 14 days.

Summary checklists

Things to be created or adopted

- None.

Procedures to be created or implemented

- Change the notice period for the AGM from the statutory 14 days to 20 working days.
- At the AGM, the chairmen of the Nomination, Remuneration and Audit Committees should attend.
- A resolution for the adoption of the accounts in the Annual Report should always be tabled to shareholders for their vote.
- Resolutions proposed at AGM should be clearly distinct on each issue, and not confusingly combined.

Disclosures to be undertaken

- The Chairman should announce the results of the proxy votes after each 'show of hands' vote.

See:

None

Score Chart

Figure 24.1 on the following page is a chart for this section of the Code.

Please refer to *Scoring Chart – ACCEPTS™ Method Instructions* (on page 53).

Following the above instructions, complete this chart first, then transcribe your results to the *Grand Score Chart* on page 197.

Excel® spreadsheet

An integrated Excel® spreadsheet model of all the individual score sheets and the *Grand Score Chart* (on page 197) is enclosed with this book.

D	RELATIONS WITH SHAREHOLDERS	Chapter 24
D.2	Constructive Use Of The AGM	

Principle:
The Board should use the AGM to communicate with investors and to encourage their participation.

Code Provisions			Date							Appendix	
		Compliance	1	-	-	-	-	-	-		1 = "Yes" 0 = "No"
D.2.1	The company should count all proxy votes and, except where a poll is called, should indicate the level of proxies lodged on each resolution, and the balance for and against the resolution and the number of abstentions, after it has been dealt with on a show of hands. The company should ensure that votes cast are properly received and recorded.	Steps Taken									
Code Provisions											
		Compliance	1	-	-	-	-	-	-		1 = "Yes" 0 = "No"
D.2.2	The company should propose a separate resolution at the AGM on each substantially separate issue and should in particular propose a resolution at the AGM relating to the report and accounts.	Steps Taken									
Code Provisions											
		Compliance	1	-	-	-	-	-	-		1 = "Yes" 0 = "No"
D.2.3	The chairman should arrange for the chairmen of the audit, remuneration and Nomination Committees to be available to answer questions at the AGM and for all directors to attend.	Steps Taken									
Code Provisions											
		Compliance	1	-	-	-	-	-	-		1 = "Yes" 0 = "No"
D.2.4	The company should arrange for the Notice of the AGM and related papers to be sent to shareholders at least 20 working days before the meeting.	Steps Taken									

Figure 24.1

RESULTS

		Compliance								
The number of **complete provisions** complied with.	a	Provisions	4	.	.	.	.	.	.	-To Summary sheet
The number of **components** complied with.	b	Components	4	.	.	.	.	.	.	-To Summary sheet

		% Compliance							
Compliance rate for **complete provisions**.	a/c	Provisions	100%	.	.	.	.	.	.
Compliance rate for **components**.	b/d	Components	100%	.	.	.	.	.	.

Figure 24.1 *Continued*

How Did You Do?

Review where you are

If you have read through each section you will now have seen all the substantive demands of the Code. There is nothing complicated in what is required, it is a series of best-practice procedures and disclosures that should be adopted.

You may have chosen to read through each section from Chapters 11–24 without completing the Score Chart. This is fine, but you need to go back through the Score Charts and complete them.

It is important to do this for two reasons.

First, to become familiar with the *ACCEPTS*™ *Method* (**A**ccelerated **C**ombined **C**ode **E**nabling **P**lan and **T**racking **S**ystem).
Second, to establish your starting point.

After completing the Score Sheet in each chapter, transcribe your results into the corresponding columns on the Grand Score Chart on page 197.

Once the first column of the Grand Score Chart is completed, it will be clear how much needs to be done in each of the Code sections. This is your initial survey.

What do my results mean?

Most companies approaching this project will achieve 'string vest' compliance – there are lots of threads, but little coverage.

You are likely to have complied with a low number of whole provisions, but sprinklings of components all over the place. This is quite normal.

Expecting a score of 5–15% of provisions, and 10–20% of components on your first evaluation exercise is realistic.

A word of encouragement

Substantially raising your initial scores may seem daunting, but there are many easy wins amongst the listed 48 provisions and 84 components.

The purpose of this book is to help you focus on sequentially completing coherent sections of the Code so that your business will reap the benefits of compliance in a future valuation.

It is not imperative that you get everything done this week! After you have completed your initial survey, it becomes apparent how much needs to be done in each compliance area.

Your priorities are very likely to be influenced by the number and nature of the NEDs you recruit.

See:

Chapter 10: Basic Steps.

Compliance - Provisions

				Date	%		%		%		%		%		%		%
A	Directors		Provisions	22	100%	.	.	.	.	.	.	.	.	.	.	.	.
B	Remuneration		Provisions	10	100%	.	.	.	.	.	.	.	.	.	.	.	.
C	Financial Reporting & Audit		Provisions	10	100%	.	.	.	.	.	.	.	.	.	.	.	.
D	Shareholders		Provisions	6	100%	.	.	.	.	.	.	.	.	.	.	.	.
	TOTAL PROVISIONS COMPLIANCE			48	100%	.	.	.	.	.	.	.	.	.	.	.	.

		CHAPTER															
A.1	The Board	11	Provisions	5	100%	.	.	.	.	.	.	.	.	.	.	.	.
A.2	Chairman & Chief Executive	12	Provisions	2	100%	.	.	.	.	.	.	.	.	.	.	.	.
A.3	Board Balance and Independence	13	Provisions	3	100%	.	.	.	.	.	.	.	.	.	.	.	.
A.4	Appointments To The Board	14	Provisions	6	100%	.	.	.	.	.	.	.	.	.	.	.	.
A.5	Information and Professional Development	15	Provisions	3	100%	.	.	.	.	.	.	.	.	.	.	.	.
A.6	Performance Evaluation	16	Provisions	1	100%	.	.	.	.	.	.	.	.	.	.	.	.
A.7	Re-election	17	Provisions	2	100%	.	.	.	.	.	.	.	.	.	.	.	.
B.1	Remuneration - The Level & Make-Up	18	Provisions	6	100%	.	.	.	.	.	.	.	.	.	.	.	.
B.2	Remuneration - Procedure	19	Provisions	4	100%	.	.	.	.	.	.	.	.	.	.	.	.
C.1	Financial Reporting	20	Provisions	2	100%	.	.	.	.	.	.	.	.	.	.	.	.
C.2	Internal Control	21	Provisions	1	100%	.	.	.	.	.	.	.	.	.	.	.	.
C.3	Audit Committee & Auditors	22	Provisions	7	100%	.	.	.	.	.	.	.	.	.	.	.	.
D.1	Dialogue With Institutional Shareholders	23	Provisions	2	100%	.	.	.	.	.	.	.	.	.	.	.	.
D.2	Constructive Use Of The AGM	24	Provisions	4	100%	.	.	.	.	.	.	.	.	.	.	.	.
	TOTAL PROVISIONS COMPLIANCE			48	100%	.	.	.	.	.	.	.	.	.	.	.	.

Compliance - Components

				Date	%	0-Jan-00	%	0-Jan-00	%	0-Jan-00	%	0-Jan-00	%	0-Jan-00	%	0-Jan-00	%
A	Directors		Components	45	100%	.	.	.	.	.	.	.	.	.	.	.	.
B	Remuneration		Components	14	100%	.	.	.	.	.	.	.	.	.	.	.	.
C	Financial Reporting & Audit		Components	19	100%	.	.	.	.	.	.	.	.	.	.	.	.
D	Shareholders		Components	6	100%	.	.	.	.	.	.	.	.	.	.	.	.
	TOTAL COMPONENTS COMPLIANCE			84	100%	.	.	.	.	.	.	.	.	.	.	.	.

		CHAPTER															
A.1	The Board	11	Components	10	100%	.	.	.	.	.	.	.	.	.	.	.	.
A.2	Chairman & Chief Executive	12	Components	3	100%	.	.	.	.	.	.	.	.	.	.	.	.
A.3	Board Balance and Independence	13	Components	11	100%	.	.	.	.	.	.	.	.	.	.	.	.
A.4	Appointments To The Board	14	Components	12	100%	.	.	.	.	.	.	.	.	.	.	.	.
A.5	Information and Professional Development	15	Components	3	100%	.	.	.	.	.	.	.	.	.	.	.	.
A.6	Performance Evaluation	16	Components	1	100%	.	.	.	.	.	.	.	.	.	.	.	.
A.7	Re-election	17	Components	5	100%	.	.	.	.	.	.	.	.	.	.	.	.
B.1	Remuneration - The Level & Make-Up	18	Components	7	100%	.	.	.	.	.	.	.	.	.	.	.	.
B.2	Remuneration - Procedure	19	Components	7	100%	.	.	.	.	.	.	.	.	.	.	.	.
C.1	Financial Reporting	20	Components	2	100%	.	.	.	.	.	.	.	.	.	.	.	.
C.2	Internal Control	21	Components	2	100%	.	.	.	.	.	.	.	.	.	.	.	.
C.3	Audit Committee & Auditors	22	Components	15	100%	.	.	.	.	.	.	.	.	.	.	.	.
D.1	Dialogue With Institutional Shareholders	23	Components	2	100%	.	.	.	.	.	.	.	.	.	.	.	.
D.2	Constructive Use Of The AGM	24	Components	4	100%	.	.	.	.	.	.	.	.	.	.	.	.
	TOTAL COMPONENTS COMPLIANCE			84	100%	.	.	.	.	.	.	.	.	.	.	.	.

Figure 25.1 Grand Score Chart

What to Do Now?

Initial review

For the reasons set out in Chapter 25 '*How Did You Do*?', you should complete your initial survey.

The process of undertaking this survey will clarify a great deal of the spirit of the Code to you. Your subsequent judgements on the priorities you select will be better informed and more effective for your business.

Remember, the Code is a framework. You and your Board must satisfy yourselves that you can claim compliance in each section based on reasonable judgement. The Code is not prescriptive in absolute specifics. When you believe you have become compliant in any section, ask yourself if your auditors would agree with you.

So, where should you start?

An essential requirement

The Board must commit to a number of actions, so it is imperative that you have got their full agreement and support for this project.

The Board itself may change radically, depending on how many NEDs are recruited and particularly when a NED Chairman is appointed. This is the most obvious outward signal of the CG metamorphosis that is taking place.

Proof of commitment of the Board is the 'green light' to recruit your first NED and to deal with the shortfall in Company Secretarial resource and quality.

Refer to the *Map of Code CG Requirements* on page 202 to gain an overview of the choices of areas to address. Each of the relevant chapters in the book are referenced.

Map of Code CG Requirements

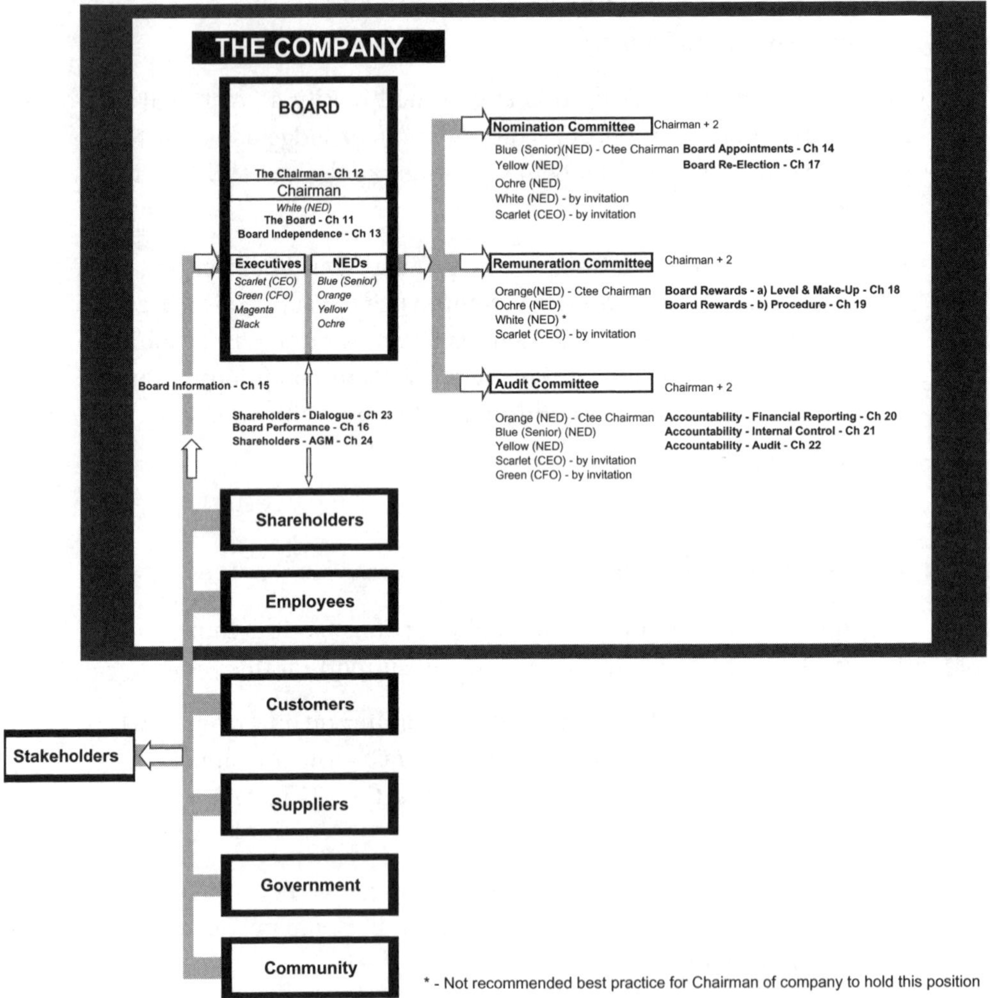

Figure 26.1

Plan of attack – preparation

- Consider how much time you have before the 'exit' event, whether trade sale or flotation. If it's happening next week, you're too late. If you plan to have 2 or 3 years, that is about right.
- Gain the commitment of the Board to embark on the CG project. Use the value-enhancing arguments set out in the early chapters, which also point out the pros and cons of doing or not doing this.

There are plenty of sceptics to pour cold water on your plan. For an array of rebuttals, see Chapter 2: No CG Recognition – The Company You Keep.

- Ensure the decision to embark on the project is made for good commercial reasons. This will be the main theme you will have to return to if the Board gets cold feet later.
- Get the NED recruitment programme under way immediately. If you aim to fill the Chairman's position first be very careful in your choice for this key position. Remember that if you are new to engaging NEDs, the Chairman may be extremely useful in assisting your CG progress.

  See:

  Chapter 13: Board Balance;

  Appendix 5: Guidance on the Role of Non-Executive Director; and

  Appendix 6: Sample Letter of Non-Executive Director Appointment.
- Review the quality of your Company Secretarial advice and be prepared to improve it. A good Company Secretary can implement and manage this project for you.

  See:

  Appendix 15: CG Role of the Company Secretary.
- Always remember the independence constraint, otherwise the value of what you are doing will be decimated.

Plan of attack – the Board itself

- Create a schedule of Board meetings for the next 15 months.
- Review the ICSA list of matters reserved for the Board and tailor it to your own needs, placing emphasis as appropriate for your business.

  See:

  Appendix 2: Matters Reserved for the Board.
- Each Board agenda item should be accompanied by a Board paper, where possible. This is extremely good discipline. It ensures the Board is better informed and is more effective in its decision-making.

  A planner for Board meetings should also include a latest date for circulation of Board papers (one or two weeks before the meeting).

- Minutes of Board meetings and Board Committees to be maintained to a high standard. It is one of the few Board obligations under the Companies Acts.
- A list of duties for the Chairman and for the Chief Executive Officer should be defined upon recruitment of an independent Chairman. Both lists of duties should be agreed by the Board.

  See:

  Appendix 3: The Role of the Chairman; and
  Appendix 4: The Role of the Chief Executive.
- If not already in place, a Directors & Officers insurance policy should be implemented.
- At a later stage, the Board should consider a method of reviewing its effectiveness.

  See:
  Appendix 10: Performance Evaluation Guidance.
- It should be apparent that these changes make the Board a much more effective, efficient and professional group. This will cause more rigorous processes to be put in place, which will percolate down through the business. This will achieve another objective of the CG project, which is to improve the quality of Board decisions being better informed.

  See:
  Chapter 15: Board Information.

Plan of attack – the Board Committees

- As the NEDs come on Board, the three cornerstone committees should be formed. These committees may be started with Executive Directors, who then step down as the NEDs are recruited.
- The sensible order of creation of the committees is Nomination, Remuneration and Audit.
- The Nomination Committee is the first to ensure a focus of effort on the recruitment of new NEDs.
- The Remuneration Committee is second, as remuneration policy and long-term incentive schemes should be addressed when enough NEDs become available.
- The Audit Committee is last because it requires the most NEDs and requires some financial experience.
- No NED should sit on all three committees.

- The ICSA recommend as a best practice that no NED should sit on both the Nomination and Remuneration Committees.
- The Chairman of the company should not be the Chairman of the Nomination or Remuneration Committees and should not be a member of the Audit Committee at all.
- The Company Secretary should be the Secretary of all the three Committees.

  For an example of how the permutations may work,

See:

Appendix 1: Annual Report – CG Disclosures; and
Page 202, Map of Code CG Requirements.

Plan of attack – the shareholders

- The main communication vehicle for the shareholders of an unquoted company is the Annual Report. Certainly, that is the normal case when share ownership extends outside the company and beyond the directors and staff. Any staff share scheme usually entails leavers.
- As the NEDs join, they should be presented to shareholders at the first available Annual General Meeting for election. Complying with these CG principles means that the Executive Directors should also be submitting to a three-year cycle of re-election.
- Shareholders should be given biographical information on the new NED(s). This will help them understand the NED's suitability and appreciate what is being brought to the Board by way of skills and experience.
- The Annual Report should be sent to shareholders with the notice of AGM. The notice for the AGM should be sent out at least 20 working days beforehand, to allow the Annual Report and accounts to be appreciated.
- The Annual Report and AGM are the 'shop window' for your CG initiative. Once your Board is committed to going down this path, it should be heavily advertised – particularly to the shareholders.
- At the AGM, the Chairman should set out the CG strategy and explain the benefits, both short- and long-term, to the shareholders.
- In the Annual Report, the policy commitment to CG and its components should be laid out.

See:
Appendix 1: Annual Report – CG Disclosures.
Shareholders usually receive this well, more so when they understand the longer term implications in the protection this affords them for their investment.

Plan of attack – the financial reporting and auditors

- The Board must declare its responsibility for the production of financial statements in the Annual Report. The auditors should do likewise. If your auditors are a 'quality' firm, they will have the Board sign off a Management Letter acknowledging these responsibilities and this will be stated in your Annual Report.
- If your company intends to sell, partially sell or float then it is worth ensuring you get a 'Big Four' audit firm.[1] Their experience is useful and their name on the audit report carries weight.
  This is not a slur against smaller audit firms, but simply a realistic defence against the potential bias of your future buyer.
- Ensure that the financial statements you produce for shareholders are intelligible and informative. You have a duty not to deliberately obscure or complicate the picture presented. In fact, under CG guidance, you have a duty to make the picture presented even clearer and more accessible.
- Before the Audit Committee is formed, the auditors are the only safety net for your shareholders. Normally, there are issues that arise during the audit process that are explained and dealt with by various officers of the company. Conflicts on policy matters, such as contract revenue recognition or Research & Development capitalization, are resolved along the way.
  The Audit Committee has a clear role to independently review such 'conflicts' amongst the NED members, the external auditors, any internal auditors and (usually) the invited Chief Executive and Chief Financial Officers. The Audit Committee now acts as a second line of reason for your shareholders.

---

[1] As an aside, Arthur Andersen used to be one of the 'Big Five' in the world of audit, so general perceptions aren't always right. The remaining 'Big Four', are PriceWaterhouseCoopers (PWC), Ernst & Young, KPMG and Deloittes.

- The Audit Committee should consider the independence of the external auditors, reviewing any non-audit work they do. There is a paradox here. You would probably choose a 'Big Four' firm because they have the experience to help you through your sale or flotation process. In the event of this happening, the balance between audit work and non-audit work will become highly skewed. This is largely unavoidable and will certainly not recur if a flotation takes place, since you only do that once! If it is a trade sale that occurs, there will be plenty of the buyer's accountants and lawyers crawling all over your business, undertaking due-diligence work. They will keep your auditors honest!
- If your business does not have an internal audit function, this should be considered in recognition of internal control obligations.
- Risk Management is a further aspect of the Board's broader responsibilities and the Audit Committee should discharge those through Business Continuity planning.

Annual Report – CG Disclosures

Annual report section: Directors, officers and advisors

Directors

M P D White (Chairman – non-executive)

R E Blue (Deputy Chairman – senior non-executive)

Dr D G Orange (non-executive)

Dr P Yellow (non-executive)

S Ochre (non-executive)

Dr A J Scarlet (Chief Executive) (appointed 12 January 2006)

N V Green (Chief Financial Officer)

J A Magenta (Chief Operating Officer)

D T Black (Commercial Director)

Secretary

T A Spectrum

Annual report section: Corporate Governance

The Board of directors of *Pellucid plc* recognizes that an effective system of corporate governance is essential to the fulfilment of corporate responsibilities and the achievement of financial objectives. In recognition of this, the Board strives to observe high standards in corporate governance. As an unlisted company, the company does not have to comply with the revised Combined Code. However, the Board of directors believe in providing a framework establishing good corporate governance and accountability.

Therefore, the Board has set out below some of the company's procedures, which provide its framework for corporate governance.

The Board

The aim of the Board in representing the interests of the company's shareholders is to develop a successful business with the principal objective of enhancing shareholder value. In support of this, the Board meets at least 6 times during the year to retain full and effective control over the company and its business affairs and to assess the performance of the company. Each Board meeting is conducted with the senior executive management team in attendance to facilitate direct dialogue between the company's Non-Executive Directors and management.

Additionally, the Board receives updates as necessary between Board meetings.

The Board has a non-executive Chairman and a separate Chief Executive and includes 4 Non-Executive Directors (including the Chairman). The role of the Non-Executive Directors is to bring independent judgement to the Board's deliberations and decisions. The Non-Executive Directors do not have responsibility for the day-to-day management of the company; this is the responsibility of the Executive Directors and other members of the senior management team under the leadership of the Chief Executive.

The composition and effectiveness of the Board is reviewed regularly to ensure that the experience of its executive and Non-Executive Directors meet the requirements of the company and its business operations. In doing so, the Board also takes into consideration the balance of executive to Non-Executive Directors, their age and term of service. All directors have access to the services of the Company Secretary and if necessary, are entitled to receive further independent professional advice at the company's expense.

Board Committees

The Board has established Remuneration, Audit and Nomination Committees each with defined terms of reference.

Remuneration Committee

Remuneration Committee Members

Dr D G Orange (Chairman) – Non-Executive Director

S Ochre – Non-Executive Director

MPD White – Non-Executive Director

The are no executive members in this committee. Dr A J Scarlet (Chief Executive) attends committee meetings by invitation, taking no part in the discussion of his own remuneration package. No director votes on his own remuneration.

This committee makes recommendations to the Board on an overall remuneration package for each executive and Non-Executive Director. The committee met three times last year.

Remuneration policy

The company's policy on Executive Directors' remuneration is that the overall remuneration package should be sufficiently competitive to attract, retain and motivate high quality executives capable of achieving the group's objectives and thereby enhancing shareholder value.

The package consists of basic salary, benefits, share options, performance-related bonuses and pensions, with a significant proportion based on performance and dependent upon achieving demanding targets. Details of directors' remuneration, share options and participation in long-term incentive plans are set out in the directors' report and notes 8 and 18 of the financial statements.

The Board believes the level of remuneration of its Non-Executive Directors is fair in relation to the responsibilities and time commitments involved and that the level of remuneration does not preclude them from acting independently.

Consideration is given to pay and employment policies elsewhere in the group, especially when determining annual salary increases.

Audit Committee

Audit Committee Members

Dr D G Orange (Chairman) – Non-Executive Director

R E Blue – senior Non-Executive Director

Dr P Yellow – Non-Executive Director

The Audit Committee meetings are also attended by the external auditors, KMPWC Ernst & Deloitte, and if requested by the committee any Executive Directors (normally CEO and CFO) and other employees.

The main responsibilities of the Board Audit Committee are:

- To review and advise the Board on the annual financial statements.
- To review with the external auditors the nature and scope of their audit.
- To review resultant issues from external audit and management's response.
- To make recommendations as to the appointment and remuneration of external auditors.
- To make recommendations regarding the resignation or removal of external auditors.
- To review the company's systems and practices for the identification and management of risk.
- To monitor internal compliance with company policies.
- To monitor external compliance with prevailing laws and regulations, commercial or otherwise.

The external auditors are appointed annually at the Annual General Meeting. The Board Audit Committee considers the re-appointment of the external auditors on the basis of performance, cost and independence and reports its findings to the Board.

The audit firm provides non-audit work, consisting largely of corporate taxation advice.

Nomination Committee

Nomination Committee Members

R E Blue (Chairman) – senior Non-Executive Director

Dr P Yellow – Non-Executive Director

S Ochre – Non-Executive Director

The committee is entirely made up of Non-Executive Directors. The company Chairman, M P D White, attends by invitation – as does Dr A J Scarlet – Chief Executive (appointed 12 January 2006).

The main responsibilities of the Board Nomination Committee are:

- To consider and make recommendations to the Board about the appointment of directors.

- To make recommendations as to the composition and structure of the Board.
- To make recommendations, if any, regarding the rotation and re-appointment of directors at general meetings of the members.

The Nomination Committee met three times during the year.

Other duties of the Chairman

Mr M P D White is the Chairman of the Board. He is a Non-Executive Director and was deemed to be independent on appointment, in accordance with the provisions of the Combined Code (A.2.2 & A.3.1). His other major professional commitment is in the capacity of Chief Executive Officer of Technology Challenges plc, a quoted company.

Executive Directors

The Chief Financial Officer, Mr N V Green, is a Non-Executive Director of Fledgling Industries plc. Pellucid plc is paid a fee for Mr Green's services by Fledgling Industries plc.

Internal control

The Board maintains full control and direction over appropriate strategic, financial, organizational and compliance issues, and has put in place an organizational structure with formally defined lines of responsibility and delegation of authority. The Board has delegated to the senior management team the implementation of the systems of internal financial control within an established framework that applies throughout the company. An internal control framework can only provide reasonable not absolute assurance against material misstatement or loss. The directors are not aware of any significant weakness or deficiencies in the company's system of internal control.

Going concern

The directors have reviewed the company's budgets and forecasts to 31 May 2008. After taking into consideration the cash flow implications of these plans, the directors are satisfied that it is appropriate to produce the financial statements on a going concern basis.

Board responsibilities for producing the accounts

The directors have reviewed the company's budgets and forecasts to 31 May 2008. After taking into consideration the cash flow implications of these plans, the directors are satisfied that it is appropriate to produce the financial statements on a going concern basis.

Auditor responsibilities

The directors have reviewed the company's budgets and forecasts to 31 May 2008. After taking into consideration the cash flow implications of these plans, the directors are satisfied that it is appropriate to produce the financial statements on a going concern basis.

Matters Reserved for the Board

ICSA Guidance Note

Reference Number

031119

ICSA Guidance Note

ICSA Guidance Note

Matters Reserved for the Board

No matter how effective a Board of directors may be it is not possible for the directors to have hands on involvement in every area of the company's business. An effective Board controls the business but delegates day to day responsibility to the executive management. That said there are a number of matters which are required to be or, in the interests of the company, should only be decided by the Board of directors as a whole. It is incumbent upon the Board to make it clear what these **Matters Reserved for the Board** are. The Combined Code states that "There should be a formal schedule of matters specifically reserved for [the Board's] decision"[1] and that the annual report should contain a "high level statement of which types of decisions are to be taken by the Board and which are to be delegated to management."[1]

The Combined Code also states that "The Board's role is to provide entrepreneurial leadership of the company within a framework of prudent and effective controls which enables risk to be assessed and managed. The Board should set the company's strategic aims, ensure that the necessary financial and human resources are in place for the company to meet its objectives and review management performance. The Board should set

[1] *The Combined Code on Corporate Governance* – July 2003, A1.1

the company's values and standards and ensure that its obligations to its shareholders and others are understood and met."[2]

ICSA has produced this Guidance Note to aid directors and company secretaries in drawing up such a schedule of Matters Reserved for the Board. The original version of this document was first published in the February 1993 edition of The Company Secretary and has been adopted as a precedent by a number of writers on corporate governance. It has been updated to incorporate more recent developments in best practice.

The relative importance of some matters included in this Guidance Note will vary according to the size and nature of the company's business. For example all companies will have a different view on the establishment of the financial limits for transactions which should be referred to the Board. Equally, there may well be items not mentioned in the Guidance Note which some companies (for example those subject to additional forms of external regulation) would wish to include in their own schedule.

Multiple signatures

In drawing up a schedule of Matters Reserved for the Board, companies should clarify which transactions require multiple Board signatures on the relevant documentation.

---

[2] *The Combined Code on Corporate Governance* – July 2003 A.1, first supporting principle

Reference Number
031119

Delegation

Certain of the matters included in this Guidance Note should, under the provisions of the Combined Code, be the subject of recommendations by the audit, nomination or remuneration committee. However, full delegation is not normally permitted in these cases as the final decision on the matter is required to be taken by the whole Board.

Urgent matters

In drawing up a schedule of Matters Reserved for the Board it is important to establish procedures for dealing with matters which often have to be dealt with urgently, often between regular Board meetings. It is recommended that a telephone or video conference meeting should be held in which as many directors as possible participate. This allows directors the opportunity to discuss the matter and ask questions. Any director who cannot attend should still be sent the relevant papers and have the opportunity to give their views to the Chairman, another director or the Company Secretary before the meeting. If the matter is routine and discussion is not necessary the approval of all the directors may be obtained by means of a written resolution. In all cases however the procedures should balance the need for urgency with the overriding principle that each director should be given as much information as possible, the time to consider it properly and an opportunity to discuss the matter prior to the commitment of the company.

The following schedule has been produced to assist Boards of directors and company secretaries in

ICSA Guidance Note

Reference Number
031119

preparing a schedule of Matters Reserved for the Board in accordance with good corporate governance.

Items marked * are not considered suitable for delegation to a committee of the Board, for example because of Companies Act requirements or because, under the recommendations of the Combined Code, they are the responsibility of an audit, nomination or remuneration committee, with the final decision required to be taken by the Board as a whole.

CA refers to the Companies Act 1985

CC refers to the Combined Code

LR refers to the UKLA Listing Rules

References to Audit, Nomination or Remuneration refer to the Board committee which will consider the item and make recommendations to the board for its final decision.

SCHEDULE OF MATTERS RESERVED FOR THE BOARD

1. Strategy and Management

1.1 Responsibility for the overall management of the group.

1.2 Approval of the group's long term objectives and commercial strategy.

1.3 Approval of the annual operating and capital expenditure budgets and any material changes to them.

Reference Number

031119

1.4 Oversight of the group's operations ensuring:

- competent and prudent management
- sound planning
- an adequate system of internal control
- adequate accounting and other records
- compliance with statutory and regulatory obligations.

1.5 Review of performance in the light of the group's strategy, objectives, business plans and budgets and ensuring that any necessary corrective action is taken. CC A.1

1.6 Extension of the group's activities into new business or geographic areas.

1.7 Any decision to cease to operate all or any material part of the group's business.

2. Structure and capital

2.1 Changes relating to the group's capital structure including reduction of capital, share issues (except under employee share plans), share buy backs [including the use of treasury shares].

2.2 Major changes to the group's corporate structure.

2.3 Changes to the group's management and control structure.

2.4 Any changes to the company's listing or its status as a plc.

3. Financial reporting and controls

3.1 *Approval of preliminary announcements of interim and final results. CC C.1 Audit

ICSA Guidance Note

Reference Number
031119

INTERNATIONAL

3.2 *Approval of the annual report and accounts, [including the corporate governance statement and remuneration report][3].

3.3 *Approval of the dividend policy.

3.4 *Declaration of the interim dividend and recommendation of the final dividend[3].

3.5 *Approval of any significant changes in accounting policies or practices.

3.6 Approval of treasury policies [including foreign currency exposure and the use of financial derivatives].

4. Internal controls

4.1. Ensuring maintenance of a sound system of internal control and risk management including:

- receiving reports on, and reviewing the effectiveness of, the group's risk and control processes to support its strategy and objectives
- undertaking an annual assessment of these processes
- approving an appropriate statement for inclusion in the annual report.

5. Contracts

5.1 Major capital projects.

5.2 Contracts which are material strategically or by reason of size, entered into by the company [or any

[3] These items are often considered by the whole Board but with the final formal decision being delegated to a committee (set up solely for that purpose). This allows time for any changes requested at the Board meeting to be incorporated into the final document before publication.

Reference Number
031119

INTERNATIONAL

subsidiary] in the ordinary course of business, for example bank borrowings [above £xx million] and acquisitions or disposals of fixed assets [above £xx million].

5.3 Contracts of the company [or any subsidiary] not in the ordinary course of business, for example loans and repayments [above £xx million]; foreign currency transactions [above £xx million]; major acquisitions or disposals [above £xx million].

5.4 Major investments [including the acquisition or disposal of interests of more than (5) percent in the voting shares of any company or the making of any takeover offer].

6. Communication

6.1 Approval of resolutions and corresponding documentation to be put forward to shareholders at a general meeting. LR 14.1

6.2 *Approval of all circulars and listing particulars [approval of routine documents such as periodic circulars about scrip dividend procedures or exercise of conversion rights could be delegated to a committee]. LR 14.1 16.1 5.2

6.3 *Approval of press releases concerning matters decided by the Board.

7. Board membership and other appointments

7.1 *Changes to the structure, size and composition of the Board, following recommendations from the nomination committee. Nomination

7.2 *Ensuring adequate succession planning for the Board and senior management. CC A.4, A.7

ICSA Guidance Note

Reference Number
031119

7.3 Appointments to the Board, following recommendations by the nomination committee. CA Nomina

7.4 *Selection of the Chairman of the Board and the Chief Executive. Nomina

7.5 *Appointment of the Senior Independent Director. CC Nomin

7.6 *Membership and Chairmanship of Board committees. Nomin

7.7 *Continuation in office of directors at the end of their term of office, when they are due to be re-elected by shareholders at the AGM and otherwise as appropriate. Nomin

7.8 *Continuation in office of any director at any time, including the suspension or termination of service of an executive director as an employee of the ompany, subject to the law and their service contract. Nomir

7.9 *Appointment or removal of the company secretary. CA s286, CC

7.10 *Appointment, reappointment or removal of the external auditor to be put to shareholders for approval, following the recommendation of the audit committee. CA CC

7.11 Appointments to boards of subsidiaries.

8. Remuneration

8.1 *Determining the remuneration policy for the directors, company secretary and other senior executives. Remune

Reference Number
031119

ICSA
INTERNATIONAL

8.2 Determining the remuneration of the non executive directors, subject to the articles of association and shareholder approval as appropriate. CC B.2.3

8.3 *The introduction of new share incentive plans or major changes to existing plans, to be put to shareholders for approval. Remuneration

9. Delegation of Authority

9.1 *The division of responsibilities between the chairman, the chief executive [and other executive directors,] which should be in writing. CC A.2.1

9.2 *Approval of terms of reference of Board committees. CC A.4.1 B.2.1, C.3.1

9.3 *Receiving reports from Board committees on their activities.

10. Corporate governance matters

10.1 *Undertaking a formal and rigorous review [annually] of its own performance, that of its committees and individual directors. CC A.6

10.2 *Determining the independence of directors. CC A.3.1

10.3 *Considering the balance of interests between shareholders, employees, customers and the community.

10.4 Review of the group's overall corporate governance arrangements.

10.5 *Receiving reports on the views of the company's shareholders. CC D.1.1

ICSA Guidance Note

Reference Number
031119

INTERNATIONAL

11. Policies

11.1 Approval of policies, including:

- Code of Conduct
- Share dealing code
- Health and safety policy
- Environmental policy
- Communications policy [including procedures for the release of price sensitive information]
- Corporate social responsibility policy
- Charitable donations policy.

12. Other

12.1 The making of political donations.

12.2 Approval of the appointment of the group's principal professional advisers.

12.3 Prosecution, defence or settlement of litigation [involving above £xx million or being otherwise material to the interests of the group].

12.4 Approval of the overall levels of insurance for the group including Directors' & Officers' liability insurance [and indemnification of directors].

12.5 Major changes to the rules of the group's pension scheme, or changes of trustees or [when this is subject to the approval of the company] changes in the fund management arrangements.

12.6 This schedule of matters reserved for Board decisions.

Reference Number
031119

Matters which the Board considers suitable for delegation are contained in the terms of reference of its Committees.

In addition, the Board will receive reports and recommendations from time to time on any matter which it considers significant to the Group.

Appendix 3

The Role of the Chairman

The Chairman is pivotal in creating the conditions for overall Board and individual director effectiveness, both inside and outside the boardroom. Specifically, it is the responsibility of the Chairman to:

- run the Board and set its agenda. The agenda should take full account of the issues and the concerns of all Board members. Agendas should be forward looking and concentrate on strategic matters rather than formulaic approvals of proposals which can be the subject of appropriate delegated powers to management;
- ensure that the members of the Board receive accurate, timely and clear information, in particular about the company's performance, to enable the Board to take sound decisions, monitor effectively and provide advice to promote the success of the company;
- ensure effective communication with shareholders and ensure that the members of the Board develop an understanding of the views of the major investors;
- manage the Board to ensure that sufficient time is allowed for discussion of complex or contentious issues, where appropriate arranging for informal meetings beforehand to enable thorough preparation for the Board discussion. It is particularly important that Non-Executive Directors have sufficient time to consider critical issues and are not faced with unrealistic deadlines for decision-making;
- take the lead in providing a properly constructed induction programme for new directors that is comprehensive, formal and tailored, facilitated by the Company Secretary;
- take the lead in identifying and meeting the development needs of individual directors, with the Company Secretary having a key role in facilitating provision. It is the responsibility of the Chairman to address the development needs of the Board as a whole with a view to enhancing its overall effectiveness as a team;
- ensure that the performance of individuals and of the Board as a whole and its committees is evaluated at least once a year; and
- encourage active engagement by all the members of the Board.

The effective Chairman:

- upholds the highest standards of integrity and probity;
- sets the agenda, style and tone of Board discussions to promote effective decision-making and constructive debate;

- promotes effective relationships and open communication, both inside and outside the boardroom, between Non-Executive Directors and executive team;
- builds an effective and complementary Board, initiating change and planning succession in Board appointments, subject to Board and shareholders' approval;
- promotes the highest standards of corporate governance and seeks compliance with the provisions of the Code wherever possible;
- ensures clear structure for and the effective running of Board committees;
- ensures effective implementation of Board decisions;
- establishes a close relationship of trust with the Chief Executive, providing support and advice while respecting executive responsibility; and
- provides coherent leadership of the company, including representing the company and understanding the views of shareholders.

Source: The Combined Code on Corporate Governance – July 2003; Higgs guidance

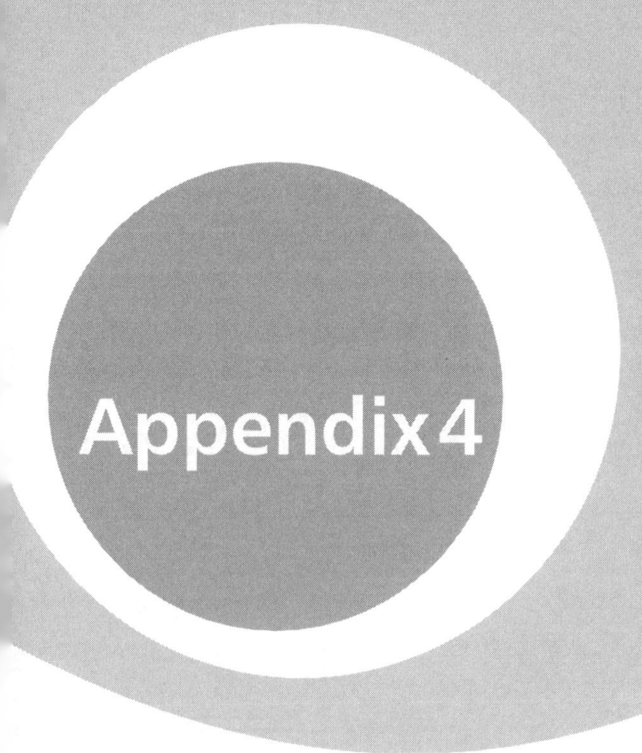

The Role of the Chief Executive

The Chief Executive is the most senior full-time executive of the company (except when there is an executive Chairman).

The Chief Executive is responsible for the performance of the company, as dictated by the Board's overall strategy. He or she reports to the Chairman or Board of directors.

Responsibilities include:

- Formulating and successfully implementing company policy;
- Directing strategy towards the profitable growth and operation of the company;
- Developing strategic operating plans that reflect the longer term objectives and priorities established by the Board;
- Maintaining an ongoing dialogue with the Chairman of the Board;
- Putting in place adequate operational planning and financial control systems;
- Ensuring that the operating objectives and standards of performance are not only understood but owned by the management and other employees;
- Closely monitoring the operating and financial results against plans and budgets;
- Taking remedial action where necessary and informing the Board of significant changes;
- Maintaining the operational performance of the company;
- Monitoring the actions of the functional Board directors;
- Assuming full accountability to the Board for all company operations;
- Representing the company to major customers and professional associations; and
- Building and maintaining an effective executive team.

Source: IOD

Guidance on the Role of the Non-Executive Director

As members of the unitary Board, all directors are required to:

- Provide entrepreneurial leadership of the company within a framework of prudent and effective controls which enable risk to be assessed and managed;
- Set the company's strategic aims, ensure that the necessary financial and human resources are in place for the company to meet its objectives, and review management performance; and
- Set the company's values and standards and ensure that its obligations to its shareholders and others are understood and met.

In addition to these requirements for all directors, the role of the Non-Executive Director has the following key elements:

- Strategy. Non-Executive Directors should constructively challenge and help develop proposals on strategy.
- Performance. Non-Executive Directors should scrutinize the performance of management in meeting agreed goals and objectives, and monitor the reporting of performance.
- Risk. Non-Executive Directors should satisfy themselves on the integrity of financial information and those financial controls and systems of risk management are robust and defensible.
- People. Non-Executive Directors are responsible for determining appropriate levels of remuneration of Executive Directors, and have a prime role in appointing, and where necessary removing, Executive Directors and in succession planning.

Non-Executive Directors should constantly seek to establish and maintain confidence in the conduct of the company. They should be independent in judgement and have an enquiring mind. To be effective, Non-Executive Directors need to build recognition by executives of their contribution in order to promote openness and trust.

To be effective, Non-Executive Directors need to be well informed about the company and the external environment in which it operates, with a strong command of issues relevant to the business. A Non-Executive Director should insist on a comprehensive, formal and tailored induction. An effective induction need not be restricted to the boardroom, so consideration should be given to visiting sites and meeting senior and middle management. Once in post, an effective Non-Executive Director should seek continually to develop and refresh their knowledge and skills to ensure that their contribution to the Board remains informed and relevant.

Best practice dictates that an effective Non-Executive Director will ensure that information is provided sufficiently in advance of meetings to enable thorough consideration of the issues facing the Board. The Non-Executive Director should insist that information is sufficient, accurate, clear and timely.

An element of the role of the Non-Executive Director is to understand the views of major investors both directly and through the Chairman and the senior independent director.

The effective Non-Executive Director:

- upholds the highest ethical standards of integrity and probity;
- supports executives in their leadership of the business while monitoring their conduct;
- questions intelligently, debates constructively, challenges rigorously and decides dispassionately;
- listens sensitively to the views of others, inside and outside the Board;
- gains the trust and respect of other Board members; and
- promotes the highest standards of corporate governance and seeks compliance with the provisions of the Code wherever possible.

Source: The Combined Code on Corporate Governance – July 2003; Higgs guidance

Sample Letter of Non-Executive Director Appointment

On (date), upon the recommendation of the Nomination Committee, the Board of (company) ('the Company') has appointed you as Non-Executive Director. I am writing to set out the terms of your appointment. It is agreed that this is a contract for services and is not a contract of employment.

Appointment

Your appointment will be for an initial term of three years commencing on (date), unless otherwise terminated earlier by and at the discretion of either party upon (one month's) written notice. Continuation of your contract of appointment is contingent on satisfactory performance and re-election at forthcoming AGMs.

Non-Executive Directors are typically expected to serve two three-year terms, although the Board may invite you to serve an additional period.

Time commitment

Overall we anticipate a time commitment of (number) days per month after the induction phase. This will include attendance at (monthly) Board meetings, the AGM, (one) annual Board away day and (at least one) site visit per year. In addition, you will be expected to devote appropriate preparation time ahead of each meeting.

By accepting this appointment, you have confirmed that you are able to allocate sufficient time to meet the expectations of your role. The agreement of the Chairman should be sought before accepting additional commitments that might impact on the time you are able to devote to your role as a Non-Executive Director of the company.

Role

Non-Executive Directors have the same general legal responsibilities to the company as any other director. The Board as a whole is collectively responsible for the success of the company.

The Board:

- provides entrepreneurial leadership of the company within a framework of prudent and effective controls which enable risk to be assessed and managed;
- sets the company's strategic aims, ensures that the necessary financial and human resources are in place for the company to meet its objectives, and reviews management performance; and
- sets the company's values and standards and ensures that its obligations to its shareholders and others are understood and met.

All directors must take decisions objectively in the interests of the company.

In addition to these requirements of all directors, the role of the Non-Executive Director has the following key elements:

- Strategy. Non-Executive Directors should constructively challenge and help develop proposals on strategy;
- Performance. Non-Executive Directors should scrutinize the performance of management in meeting agreed goals and objectives and monitor the reporting of performance;
- Risk. Non-Executive Directors should satisfy themselves on the integrity of financial information and that financial controls and systems of risk management are robust and defensible; and
- People. Non-Executive Directors are responsible for determining appropriate levels of remuneration of Executive Directors and have a prime role in appointing, and where necessary removing, Executive Directors and in succession planning.

Fees

You will be paid a fee of £(amount) gross per annum which will be paid monthly in arrears, (plus (number) ordinary shares of the company per annum, both of) which will be subject to an annual review by the Board. The company will reimburse you for all reasonable and properly documented expenses you incur in performing the duties of your office.

Outside interests

It is accepted and acknowledged that you have business interests other than those of the company and have declared any conflicts that are apparent at present. In the event that you become aware of any potential conflicts of interest, these should be disclosed to the Chairman and Company Secretary as soon as apparent.

(The Board of the company has determined you to be independent according to provision A.3.1 of the Code.)

Confidentiality

All information acquired during your appointment is confidential to the company and should not be released, either during your appointment or following termination (by whatever means), to third parties without prior clearance from the Chairman.

Your attention is also drawn to the requirements under both legislation and regulation as to the disclosure of price-sensitive information. Consequently you should avoid making any statements that might risk a breach of these requirements without prior clearance from the Chairman or Company Secretary.

Induction

Immediately after appointment, the company will provide a comprehensive, formal and tailored induction. This will include the information pack recommended by the Institute of Chartered Secretaries and Administrators (ICSA), available at www.icsa.org.uk. We will also arrange for site visits and meetings with senior and middle management and the company's auditors. We will also offer to major shareholders the opportunity to meet you.

Review process

The performance of individual directors and the whole Board and its committees is evaluated annually. If, in the interim, there are any matters which cause you concern about your role you should discuss them with the Chairman as soon as is appropriate.

Insurance

The company has directors' and officers' liability insurance and it is intended to maintain such cover for the full term of your appointment. The current indemnity limit is £ (amount); a copy of the policy document is attached.

Independent professional advice

Occasions may arise when you consider that you need professional advice in the furtherance of your duties as a director. Circumstances may occur when it will be appropriate for you to seek advice from independent advisors at the company's expense. A copy of the Board's agreed procedure under which directors may obtain such independent advice is attached. The company will reimburse the full cost of expenditure incurred in accordance with the attached policy.

Committees

This letter refers to your appointment as a Non-Executive Director of the company. In the event that you are also asked to serve on one or more of the Board committees, this will be covered in a separate communication setting out the committee(s)'s terms of reference, any specific responsibilities and any additional fees that may be involved.

This sample appointment letter has been compiled with the assistance of ICSA *www.icsa.org.uk*

Source: The Combined Code on Corporate Governance – July 2003; Higgs guidance

Chairman of the Nomination Committee – Job Description

This Committee, as a matter of good practice, carries out the selection process of directors and makes recommendations to the full Board. The Chairman of the Committee should:

- Establish, maintain and develop reporting and meeting procedures for the Board and its committees;
- Determine policy for the frequency, purpose, conduct and duration of meetings;
- Create comprehensive agenda covering all the necessary and appropriate issues throughout the year, while also including important immediate issues;
- Assign tasks and objectives to individuals and agree the working relationships between them;
- Define and review regularly the information needs of the Committee;
- Adopt efficient and timely methods for informing and briefing Committee members prior to meetings;
- Maintain proper focus on the Committee's key role and tasks;
- Allow sufficient time for important matters to be discussed thoroughly;
- Encourage all Committee members to attend all Committee meetings and to contribute appropriately to discussion, drawing on the full range of relevant opinions, knowledge, skills and experience;
- Draw together the pertinent points from discussions in a timely way in order to reach well-informed decisions that command consensus;
- Ensure that adequate minutes are kept and that Committee attendance and Committee decisions are properly recorded.

Chairman of the Remuneration Committee – Job Description

As a matter of good practice, the remuneration of Executive Directors should be dealt with by a committee made up of Non-Executive Directors. The Chairman of the Committee should:

- Establish, maintain and develop reporting and meeting procedures for the Board and its committees;
- Determine policy for the frequency, purpose, conduct and duration of meetings;
- Create comprehensive agenda covering all the necessary and appropriate issues throughout the year, while also including important immediate issues;
- Assign tasks and objectives to individuals and agree the working relationships between them;
- Define and review regularly the information needs of the Committee;
- Adopt efficient and timely methods for informing and briefing Committee members prior to meetings;
- Maintain proper focus on the Committee's key role and tasks;
- Allow sufficient time for important matters to be discussed thoroughly;
- Encourage all Committee members to attend all Committee meetings and to contribute appropriately to discussion, drawing on the full range of relevant opinions, knowledge, skills and experience;
- Draw together the pertinent points from discussions in a timely way in order to reach well-informed decisions that command consensus;
- Ensure that adequate minutes are kept and that Committee attendance and Committee decisions are properly recorded.

Chairman of the Audit Committee – Job Description

This Committee is intended to provide the link between the Company's Auditors and the independent Non-Executive Directors of the Company. The Chairman of the Committee should:

- Establish, maintain and develop reporting and meeting procedures for the Board and its committees;
- Determine policy for the frequency, purpose, conduct and duration of meetings;
- Create comprehensive agenda covering all the necessary and appropriate issues throughout the year, while also including important immediate issues;
- Assign tasks and objectives to individuals and agree the working relationships between them;
- Define and review regularly the information needs of the Committee;
- Adopt efficient and timely methods for informing and briefing Committee members prior to meetings;
- Maintain proper focus on the Committee's key role and tasks;
- Allow sufficient time for important matters to be discussed thoroughly;
- Encourage all Committee members to attend all Committee meetings and to contribute appropriately to discussion, drawing on the full range of relevant opinions, knowledge, skills and experience;
- Draw together the pertinent points from discussions in a timely way in order to reach well-informed decisions that command consensus;
- Ensure that adequate minutes are kept and that Committee attendance and Committee decisions are properly recorded.

Performance Evaluation Guidance

The Code provides that the Board should undertake a formal and rigorous annual evaluation of its own performance and that of its committees and individual directors. Individual evaluation should aim to show whether each director continues to contribute effectively and to demonstrate commitment to the role (including commitment of time for Board and committee meetings and any other duties). The Chairman should act on the results of the performance evaluation by recognizing the strengths and addressing the weaknesses of the Board and, where appropriate, proposing new members be appointed to the Board or seeking the resignation of directors. The Board should state in the annual report how such performance evaluation has been conducted.

It is the responsibility of the Chairman to select an effective process and to act on its outcome. The use of an external third party to conduct the evaluation will bring objectivity to the process.

The Non-Executive Directors, led by the senior independent director, should be responsible for performance evaluation of the Chairman, taking into account the views of Executive Directors.

The evaluation process will be used constructively as a mechanism to improve Board effectiveness, maximize strengths and tackle weaknesses. The results of Board evaluation should be shared with the Board as a whole while the results of individual assessments should remain confidential between the Chairman and the Non-Executive Director concerned.

The following are some of the questions that should be considered in a performance evaluation. They are, however, by no means definitive or exhaustive and companies will wish to tailor the questions to suit their own needs and circumstances.

The responses to these questions and others should enable Boards to assess how they are performing and to identify how certain elements of their performance areas might be improved.

Performance evaluation of the Board

- How well has the Board performed against any performance objectives that have been set?
- What has been the Board's contribution to the testing and development of strategy?
- What has been the Board's contribution to ensuring robust and effective risk management?
- Is the composition of the Board and its committees appropriate, with the right mix of knowledge and skills to maximize performance in the light of future strategy?
- Are inside and outside the Board relationships working effectively?
- How has the Board responded to any problems or crises that have emerged and could or should these have been foreseen?
- Are the matters specifically reserved for the Board the right ones?
- How well does the Board communicate with the management team, company employees and others?
- How effectively does it use mechanisms such as the AGM and the Annual Report?
- Is the Board as a whole up-to-date with the latest developments in the regulatory environment and the market?
- How effective are the Board's committees?
  (Specific questions on the performance of each committee should be included such as, for example, their role, their composition and their interaction with the Board.)

The processes that help underpin the Board's effectiveness should also be evaluated, e.g.

- Is appropriate, timely information of the right length and quality provided to the Board and is management responsive to requests for clarification or amplification?
- Does the Board provide helpful feedback to management on its requirements?
- Are sufficient Board and committee meetings of appropriate length held to enable proper consideration of issues? Is time used effectively?
- Are Board procedures conducive to effective performance and flexible enough to deal with all eventualities?

In addition, there are some specific issues relating to the Chairman which should be included as part of an evaluation of the Board's performance, e.g.

- Is the Chairman demonstrating effective leadership of the Board?
- Are relationships and communications with shareholders well managed?
- Are relationships and communications within the Board constructive?
- Are the processes for setting the agenda working? Do they enable Board members to raise issues and concerns?
- Is the Company Secretary being used appropriately and to maximum value?

Performance evaluation of the Non-Executive Director

The Chairman and other Board members should consider the following issues and the individual concerned should also be asked to assess themselves. For each Non-Executive Director:

- How well prepared and informed are they for Board meetings and is their meeting attendance satisfactory?
- Do they demonstrate a willingness to devote time and effort to understand the company and its business and a readiness to participate in events outside the boardroom such as site visits?
- What has been the quality and value of their contributions at Board meetings?
- What has been their contribution to development of strategy and to risk management?
- How successfully have they brought their knowledge and experience to bear in the consideration of strategy?
- How effectively have they probed to test information and assumptions? Where necessary, how resolute are they in maintaining their own views and resisting pressure from others?
- How effectively and proactively have they followed up their areas of concern?
- How effective and successful are their relationships with fellow Board members, the Company Secretary and senior management?
- Does their performance and behaviour engender mutual trust and respect within the Board?

How actively and successfully do they refresh their knowledge and skills and are they up-to-date with:

- the latest developments in areas such as corporate governance framework and financial reporting ?
- the industry and market conditions?
- How well do they communicate with fellow Board members, senior management and others, for example shareholders? Are they able to present their views convincingly yet diplomatically and do they listen and take on-board the views of others?

Source: The Combined Code on Corporate Governance – July 2003; Higgs guidance

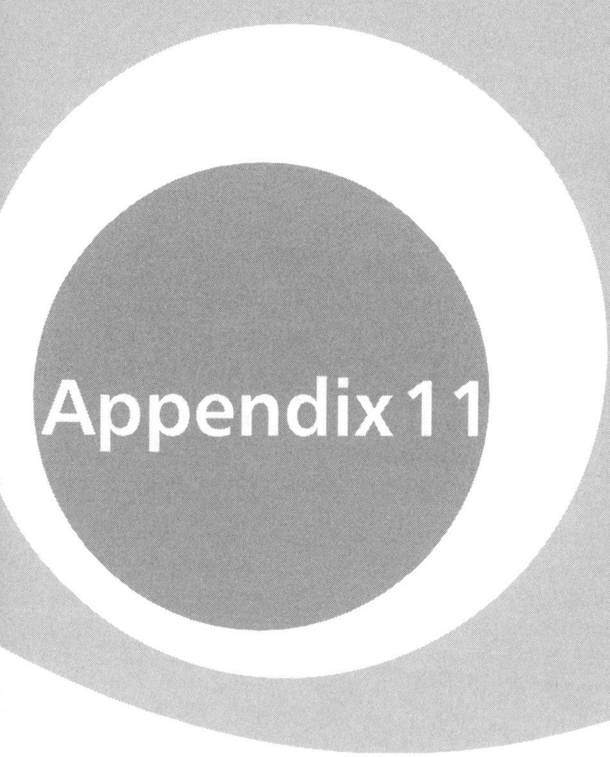

The Whistle-blowing Procedure

1. What is 'Whistle-blowing'?

It is disclosure of information by an employee, based on a reasonable belief that one or more of the following is/has/will be committed:

- A criminal offence
- A failure to comply with the law
- A miscarriage of justice
- A health and safety breach
- Environmental damage
- Concealment of any of the above.

Normal channels of reporting may be unavailable to the worker, as it may be that worker's immediate line management perpetrating the wrongdoing.

2. Why have a Whistle-blowing Procedure?

Since the advent of the Public Interest Disclosure Act (PIDA) 1998, certain protections, largely for preventing victimisation, were created for Whistle-blowers. This amended the Employment Rights Act 1996. The formal introduction of a Whistle-blowing Procedure embeds a process that may assist TAP in avoiding crises, minimizing bad press and reassuring customers and regulations advice. The FSA recommends *all* companies should have a Whistle-blowing Procedure.

3. How would a Whistle-blowing Procedure benefit your company?

It would benefit by:

- Increasing the likelihood that the company will hear about wrongdoing in time to prevent serious damage
- Reduce the amount of time and resources that would have to be diverted to managing a crisis
- Reduce the chances of workers taking concerns directly to the media
- Deterring people from engaging in malpractice, by increasing the likelihood they will be caught.

PIDA provides other persuasive reasons for having such a procedure. If a worker makes a 'wider disclosure' to the police, an MP, media, etc., there is a reasonableness test to be met for the Whistle-blower to be protected under PIDA.

Thus, if an employer had a Whistle-blowing Procedure and the worker failed to use it – it is less likely the worker would meet the reasonableness test. By the same token, the worker is more likely to use the internal procedure if it exists.

4. How would a Whistle-blowing Procedure be implemented? What would it look like?

- A clear statement from the Board that malpractice is taken seriously and citing examples of the sort of matters regarded as malpractice.
- Respect for confidentiality, if requested, and the opportunity to raise concerns outside line-management structures. This is frequently resolved by providing a private e-mail address to the Senior Non-Executive Director.
- Penalties for making false or malicious accusations.
- An indication as to how concerns may be raised outside the organization, if necessary.

5. Conclusion and recommendation

The Financial Services Authority (FSA) is the 'dad' of the UK Listings Authority (UKLA).

The FSA recommends the adoption of a Whistle-blowing Procedure by *all* companies.

In cases where staff feel compelled to expose malpractice it is better to provide a procedure than to have that person invent one. This gives a realistic chance of the company dealing with the problem itself.

If the company forcefully publicises a Whistle-blowing Procedure to staff about its view on malpractice, then it needs to practise what it preaches and be open to concerns – and respond to concerns.

I therefore recommend compliance with the FSA advice, providing a simple channel to senior management. It is sensible to nominate an 'independent' party, thus the recommendation of a Non-Executive Director.

Detailed implementation plans are outside the scope of this book, but the result of adoption of this process may mean that senior management is the first to know about serious malpractice concerns, as opposed to the last.

Nomination Committee – Terms of Reference

Terms of Reference – Nomination Committee

The Combined Code on Corporate Governance (the Combined Code) states that:

> "There should be a formal, rigorous and transparent procedure for the appointment of new directors to the board."[1]

It also provides that:

> "There should be a nomination committee which should lead the process for board appointments and make recommendations to the board."[2]

Previous guidance has permitted smaller listed companies to allow the board to act as a Nomination Committee. This is no longer the case and, although the Higgs review recognised that it may take time for smaller companies to comply, it states "there should be no differentiation in the Code's provision for larger and smaller companies."[3]

The recommendation is that companies should go through a formal process of reviewing the balance and effectiveness of its board, identifying the skills needed and those individuals who might best provide them. In particular the committee must assess the time commitments of the board posts and ensure that the individual has sufficient available time to undertake them.

As with most aspects of corporate governance, however, the company must be seen to be doing so in a fair and thorough manner. It is, therefore, essential that a Nomination Committee be properly constituted with a clear remit and identified authority.

The Combined Code states that the majority of members of a Nomination Committee should be independent non-executive directors

---

[1] *The Combined Code on Corporate Governance* – July 2003 A.4
[2] *The Combined Code on Corporate Governance* – July 2003 A.4.1
[3] *Review of the role and effectiveness of non-executive directors* – January 2003 para. 16.8

although it gives no guidance on the overall size of the Committee. We have recommended a Committee of three but companies with larger boards may wish to consider increasing this to four or five.[4]

Although not a provision in the Combined Code, the Higgs review states as good practice, in its Non-Code Recommendations, that the company secretary (or their designee) should act as secretary to the Committee.[5] It is the company secretary's responsibility to ensure that the board and its Committees are properly constituted and advised. There also needs to be a clear co-ordination between the main board and the various Committees where the company secretary would normally act as a valued intermediary.

The frequency with which the Committee needs to meet will vary considerably from company to company and may change from time to time. It is, however, clear that it must meet close to the year-end to consider whether or not directors retiring by rotation or reaching a pre-determined age limit should be put forward for re-appointment at the Annual General Meeting (AGM) and to review the statement in the annual report concerning its activities. We would recommend that it should meet at least twice a year in order to discharge its responsibilities properly.

The list of duties we have proposed are based on those contained in the Summary of The Principal Duties of the Nomination Committee which ICSA drew up for the Higgs review, which we believe all Nomination Committees should consider. Some companies may wish to add to this list and some smaller companies may need to modify it in other ways. The Chairman of the Committee should attend the AGM prepared to respond to any questions which may be raised by shareholders on matters within the Committee's area of responsibility.[6]

---

[4] *The Combined Code on Corporate Governance* – July 2003 A.4.1. The definition of independence is given in Combined Code provision A.3.1
[5] *Review of the role and effectiveness of non-executive directors* para 11.30
[6] *The Combined Code on Corporate Governance* – July 2003 D.2.3

There is clearly a need for a guiding document for the effective operation of the Nomination Committee. This has led the ICSA to produce this Guidance Note proposing model terms of reference for a Nomination Committee. The document draws on the experience of senior Company Secretaries and best practice as carried out in some of the country's leading companies.

The Combined Code also requires that the terms of reference of the Nomination Committee, explaining its role and the authority delegated to it by the board, be made available on request and placed on the company's website.[7]

Reference to "the Committee" shall mean the Nomination Committee. Reference to "the board" shall mean the board of directors. The square brackets contain recommendations which are in line with best practice but which may need to be changed to suit the circumstances of the particular organisation.

---

1. Membership

1.1 Members of the Committee shall be appointed by the board and shall be made up of least [3] members, the majority of whom should be independent non-executive directors.

1.2 Only members of the Committee have the right to attend Committee meetings. However, other individuals such as the Chief Executive, the head of human resources and external advisers may be invited to attend for all or part of any meeting, as and when appropriate.

1.3 Appointments to the Committee shall be for a period of up to three years, which may be extended for two further three-year periods provided that the majority of the Committee members remain independent.

[7] *The Combined Code on Corporate Governance* – July 2003 A.4.1

1.4 The board shall appoint the Committee Chairman who should be either the Chairman of the board or an independent non-executive director. In the absence of the Committee Chairman and/or an appointed deputy, the remaining members present shall elect one of their number to chair the meeting. The Chairman of the board shall not chair the Committee when it is dealing with the matter of succession to the chairmanship.

2. Secretary

2.1 The company secretary or their nominee shall act as the secretary of the Committee.

3. Quorum

3.1 The quorum necessary for the transaction of business shall be [2] both of whom must be independent non-executive directors. A duly convened meeting of the Committee at which a quorum is present shall be competent to exercise all or any of the authorities, powers and discretions vested in or exercisable by the Committee.

4. Frequency of Meetings

4.1 The Committee shall meet [at least twice a year][quarterly on the first Wednesday in each of January, April, July and October] and at such other times as the Chairman of the Committee shall require.[8]

5. Notice of Meetings

5.1 Meetings of the Committee shall be summoned by the secretary of the Committee at the request of the Chairman of the Committee.

[8] The frequency and timing of meetings will differ according to the needs of the company. Meetings should be organised so that attendance is maximised (for example by timetabling them to coincide with board meetings).

5.2 Unless otherwise agreed, notice of each meeting confirming the venue, time and date, together with an agenda of items to be discussed, shall be forwarded to each member of the Committee, any other person required to attend and all other non-executive directors, no later than [5] working days before the date of the meeting. Supporting papers shall be sent to Committee members and to other attendees as appropriate, at the same time.

6. Minutes of Meetings

6.1 The secretary shall minute the proceedings and resolutions of all Committee meetings, including the names of those present and in attendance.

6.2 Minutes of Committee meetings shall be circulated promptly to all members of the Committee and the Chairman of the board and, once agreed, to all other members of the board, unless a conflict of interest exists.

7. Annual General Meeting

7.1 The Chairman of the Committee shall attend the Annual General Meeting prepared to respond to any shareholder questions on the Committee's activities.

8. Duties

8.1 The Committee shall:

8.1.1 regularly review the structure, size and composition (including the skills, knowledge and experience) required of the board compared to its current position and make recommendations to the board with regard to any changes;

8.1.2 give full consideration to succession planning for directors and other senior executives in the course of its work, taking into account the challenges and

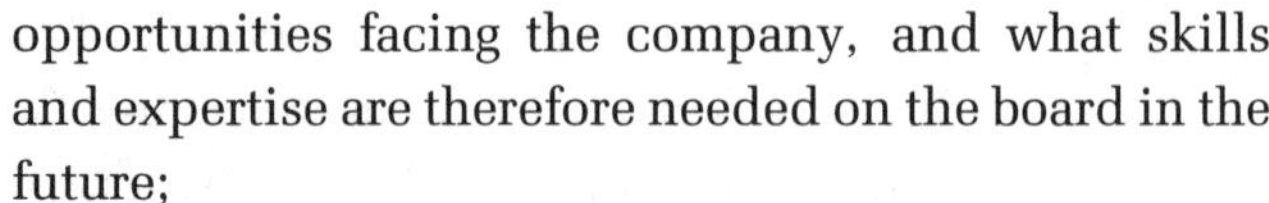

opportunities facing the company, and what skills and expertise are therefore needed on the board in the future;

8.1.3 be responsible for identifying and nominating for the approval of the board, candidates to fill board vacancies as and when they arise;

8.1.4 before appointment is made by the board, evaluate the balance of skills, knowledge and experience on the board, and, in the light of this evaluation prepare a description of the role and capabilities required for a particular appointment. In identifying suitable candidates the Committee shall:

8.1.4.1 use open advertising or the services of external advisers to facilitate the search;

8.1.4.2 consider candidates from a wide range of backgrounds; and

8.1.4.3 consider candidates on merit and against objective criteria, taking care that appointees have enough time available to devote to the position;

8.1.5 keep under review the leadership needs of the organisation, both executive and non-executive, with a view to ensuring the continued ability of the organisation to compete effectively in the marketplace;

8.1.6 keep up to date and fully informed about strategic issues and commercial changes affecting the company and the market in which it operates;

8.1.7 review annually the time required from non-executive directors. Performance evaluation should be used to assess whether the non-executive directors are spending enough time to fulfil their duties; and

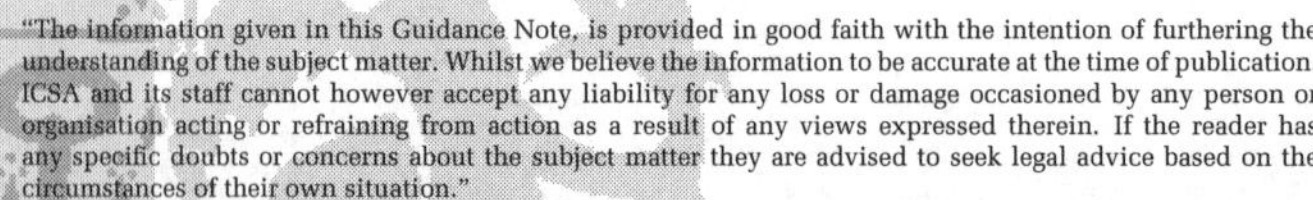

8.1.8 ensure that on appointment to the board, non-executive directors receive a formal letter of appointment setting out clearly what is expected of them in terms of time commitment, committee service and involvement outside board meetings.

8.2 The Committee shall also make recommendations to the board concerning:

8.2.1 formulating plans for succession for both executive and nonexecutive directors and in particular for the key roles of Chairman and Chief Executive (but see 8.2.8 below);

8.2.2 suitable candidates for the role of senior independent director;

8.2.3 membership of the Audit and Remuneration Committees, in consultation with the Chairmen of those committees;

8.2.4 the re-appointment of any non-executive director at the conclusion of their specified term of office having given due regard to their performance and ability to continue to contribute to the board in the light of the knowledge, skills and experience required;

8.2.5 the continuation (or not) in service of any director who has reached the age of [70];

8.2.6 the re-election by shareholders of any director under the 'retirement by rotation' provisions in the company's articles of association having due regard to their performance and ability to continue to contribute to the board in the light of the knowledge, skills and experience required;

8.2.7 any matters relating to the continuation in office of any director at any time including the suspension or termination of service of an executive director as an employee of the company subject to the provisions of the law and their service contract; and

8.2.8 the appointment of any director to executive or other office other than to the positions of Chairman and Chief Executive, the recommendation for which would be considered at a meeting of the full board.

9. Reporting Responsibilities

9.1 The Committee Chairman shall report formally to the board on its proceedings after each meeting on all matters within its duties and responsibilities.

9.2 The Committee shall make whatever recommendations to the board it deems appropriate on any area within its remit where action or improvement is needed.

9.3 The Committee shall make a statement in the annual report about its activities, the process used to make appointments and explain if external advice or open advertising has not been used.

10. Other

10.1 The Committee shall, at least once a year, review its own performance, constitution and terms of reference to ensure it is operating at maximum effectiveness and recommend any changes it considers necessary to the board for approval.

11. Authority

11.1 The Committee is authorised to seek any information it requires from any employee of the company in order to perform its duties.

11.2 The Committee is authorised to obtain, at the company's expense, outside legal or other professional advice on any matters within its terms of reference.

October 2003

Remuneration Committee – Terms of Reference

ICSA Guidance Notes

Terms of Reference – Remuneration Committee

The Combined Code on Corporate Governance (the Combined Code) states that:

> "There should be a formal and transparent procedure for developing policy on executive remuneration and for fixing the remuneration packages of individual directors."[1]

It goes on to state that:

> "The board should establish a remuneration committee ... [which] should make available its terms of reference, explaining its role and the authority delegated to it by the board."[2]

As with most aspects of corporate governance, the above principles make it clear that, not only should companies go through a formal process of considering executive remuneration, but they must be seen to be doing so in a fair and thorough manner. It is, therefore, essential that the Remuneration Committee is properly constituted with a clear remit and identified authority.

The Combined Code recommends the Committee be made up of at least three independent non-executive directors (although two is permissible for smaller companies).[3]

Although not a provision in the Combined Code, the Higgs review, states as good practice, in its Non-Code Recommendations, that the company secretary (or their designee) should act as secretary to the Committee.[4] It is the company secretary's responsibility to ensure that the board and its Committees are properly constituted and advised. There also needs to be a clear co-ordination between the main board and the various Committees where the company secretary would normally act as a valued intermediary.

---

[1] *The Combined Code on Corporate Governance* – July 2003, B.2

[2] *The Combined Code on Corporate Governance* – July 2003, B.2.1

[3] A smaller company is defined as one which is below the FTSE 350 throughout the year immediately before the reporting year.

[4] *Review of the role and effectiveness of non-executive directors,* January 2003 para 11.30

The frequency with which the Committee needs to meet will vary from company to company and may change from time to time. It is, however, clear that it must meet close to the year end; to review the Remuneration Report which is required to be prepared under the Directors' Remuneration Report Regulations 2002 and be submitted to shareholders with or as part of the company's annual report for their approval at the AGM. We would recommend that the Committee should meet at least twice a year in order to discharge its responsibilities properly.

The list of duties we have proposed are those contained within the Summary of Principle Duties of the Remuneration Committee which ICSA helped compile for the Higgs review and which are now appended to the Combined Code. Some companies may wish to add to this list and some smaller companies may need to modify it in other ways. The Combined Code also states that the Chairman of the Committee should attend the AGM prepared to respond to any questions that may be raised by shareholders on matters within the Committee's area of responsibility.[5]

There is clearly a need for there to be a guiding document for the effective operation of the Remuneration Committee. This has led the ICSA to produce this Guidance Note proposing model terms of reference for a Remuneration Committee. The document draws on the experience of senior Company Secretaries and best practice as carried out in some of the country's leading companies.

The Combined Code also requires that the terms of reference of the Remuneration Committee, explaining its role and the authority delegated to it by the board, be made available on request and placed on the company's website.[6]

References to "the Committee" shall mean the Remuneration Committee. References to "the board" shall mean the board of directors. The square brackets contain recommendations which are in line

[5] *The Combined Code on Corporate Governance* – July 2003 D.2.3
[6] *The Combined Code on Corporate Governance* – July 2002 A.4.1

with best practice but which may need to be changed to suit the circumstances of the particular organisation.

---

1. **Membership**

1.1 Members of the Committee shall be appointed by the board, on the recommendation of the Nomination Committee in consultation with the Chairman of the Remuneration Committee. The Committee shall be made up of at least [3] members, all of whom are independent non-executive directors.

1.2 Only members of the Committee have the right to attend Committee meetings. However, other individuals such as the Chief Executive, the head of human resources and external advisers may be invited to attend for all or part of any meeting as and when appropriate.

1.3 Appointments to the Committee shall be for a period of up to three years, which may be extended for two further three-year periods, provided the director remains independent.

1.4 The board shall appoint the Committee Chairman who shall be an independent non-executive director. In the absence of the Committee Chairman and/or an appointed deputy, the remaining members present shall elect one of themselves to chair the meeting. The Chairman of the board shall not be Chairman of the Committee.

2. **Secretary**

2.1 The company secretary or their nominee shall act as the secretary of the Committee.

3. **Quorum**

3.1 The quorum necessary for the transaction of business shall be [2]. A duly convened meeting of the Committee at which a quorum is present shall be competent to exercise all or

any of the authorities, powers and discretions vested in or exercisable by the Committee.

4. Meetings

4.1 The Committee shall meet [at least twice a year][quarterly on the first Wednesday in each of January, April, July and October] and at such other times as the Chairman of the Committee shall require.[7]

5. Notice of Meetings

5.1 Meetings of the Committee shall be summoned by the secretary of the Committee at the request of any of its members.

5.2 Unless otherwise agreed, notice of each meeting confirming the venue, time and date together with an agenda of items to be discussed, shall be forwarded to each member of the Committee, any other person required to attend and all other non-executive directors, no later than [5] working days before the date of the meeting. Supporting papers shall be sent to Committee members and to other attendees as appropriate, at the same time.

6. Minutes of Meetings

6.1 The secretary shall minute the proceedings and resolutions of all Committee meetings, including the names of those present and in attendance.

6.2 Minutes of Committee meetings shall be circulated promptly to all members of the Committee and, once agreed, to all members of the board, unless a conflict of interest exists.

[7] The frequency and timing of meetings will differ according to the needs of the company. Meetings should be organised so that attendance is maximised (for example by timetabling them to coincide with board meetings).

7. Annual General Meeting

7.1 The Chairman of the Committee shall attend the Annual General Meeting prepared to respond to any shareholder questions on the Committee's activities.

8. Duties

The Committee shall:

8.1 determine and agree with the board the framework or broad policy for the remuneration of the company's Chief Executive, Chairman, the executive directors, the company secretary and such other members of the executive management as it is designated to consider.[8] The remuneration of non-executive directors shall be a matter for the Chairman and the executive members of the board. No director or manager shall be involved in any decisions as to their own remuneration;

8.2 in determining such policy, take into account all factors which it deems necessary. The objective of such policy shall be to ensure that members of the executive management of the company are provided with appropriate incentives to encourage enhanced performance and are, in a fair and responsible manner, rewarded for their individual contributions to the success of the company;

8.3 review the ongoing appropriateness and relevance of the remuneration policy;

8.4 approve the design of, and determine targets for, any performance related pay schemes operated by the company and approve the total annual payments made under such schemes;

[8] Some companies require the Remuneration Committee to consider the packages of all executives at or above a specified level, such as those reporting to a main board director, while others require the Committee to deal with all packages above a certain figure.

8.5 review the design of all share incentive plans for approval by the board and shareholders. For any such plans, determine each year whether awards will be made, and if so, the overall amount of such awards, the individual awards to executive directors and other senior executives and the performance targets to be used;

8.6 determine the policy for, and scope of, pension arrangements for each executive director and other senior executives;

8.7 ensure that contractual terms on termination, and any payments made, are fair to the individual, and the company, that failure is not rewarded and that the duty to mitigate loss is fully recognised;

8.8 within the terms of the agreed policy and in consultation with the Chairman and/or Chief Executive as appropriate, determine the total individual remuneration package of each executive director and other senior executives including bonuses, incentive payments and share options or other share awards;

8.9 in determining such packages and arrangements, give due regard to any relevant legal requirements, the provisions and recommendations in the Combined Code and the UK Listing Authority's Listing Rules and associated guidance;

8.10 review and note annually the remuneration trends across the company or group;

8.11 oversee any major changes in employee benefits structures throughout the company or group;

8.12 agree the policy for authorising claims for expenses from the Chief Executive and Chairman;[9]

[9] It is suggested that the more common arrangement is for the Chairman of the board to authorise the Chief Executive's expenses and for the Chairman of the

8.13 ensure that all provisions regarding disclosure of remuneration including pensions, as set out in the Directors' Remuneration Report Regulations 2002 and the Combined Code are fulfilled; and

8.14 be exclusively responsible for establishing the selection criteria, selecting, appointing and setting the terms of reference for any remuneration consultants who advise the committee: and to obtain reliable, up-to-date information about remuneration in other companies. The Committee shall have full authority to commission any reports or surveys which it deems necessary to help it fulfil its obligations.

9. Reporting Responsibilities

9.1 The Committee Chairman shall report formally to the board on its proceedings after each meeting on all matters within its duties and responsibilities.

9.2 The Committee shall make whatever recommendations to the board it deems appropriate on any area within its remit where action or improvement is needed.

9.3 The Committee shall produce an annual report of the company's remuneration policy and practices which will form part of the company's annual report and ensure each year that it is put to shareholders for approval at the AGM.

10. Other

10.1 The Committee shall, at least once a year, review its own performance, constitution and terms of reference to ensure it is operating at maximum effectiveness and recommend any changes it considers necessary to the board for approval.

Remuneration Committee to authorise the Chairman's claims. An alternative would be for the Committee to authorise the expenses of both.

11. Authority

11.1 The Committee is authorised by the board to seek any information it requires from any employee of the company in order to perform its duties.

11.2 In connection with its duties the Committee is authorised by the board to obtain, at the company's expense, any outside legal or other professional advice.

October 2003

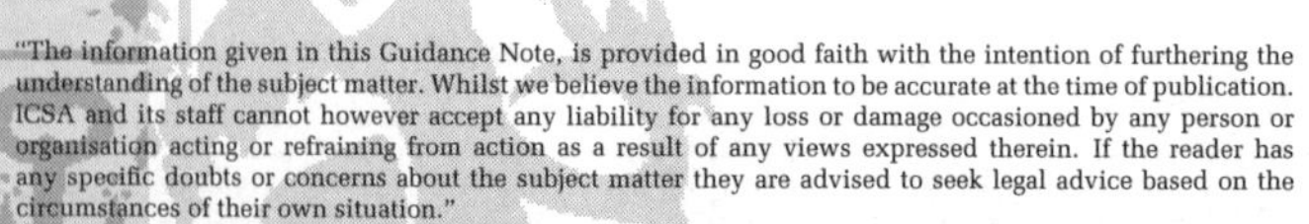

Audit Committee – Terms of Reference

ICSA Guidance Notes

Terms of Reference – Audit Committee

The Combined Code on Corporate Governance (the Combined Code) states that:

> "The board should establish formal and transparent arrangements for considering how they should apply the financial reporting and internal control principles and for maintaining an appropriate relationship with the company's auditors."[1]

The Combined Code goes on to say that the main role and responsibilities of the Audit Committee should be "set out in written terms of reference."[2] Such statements express a clear need for an Audit Committee, the requirement for which is also supported by other influential organisations such the Commonwealth Association for Corporate Governance and the International Corporate Governance Network.

The Guidance on Audit Committees (The Smith Report) recognises that "Audit committee arrangements need to be proportionate to the task, and will vary according to the size, complexity and risk profile of the company."[3]

As with most aspects of corporate governance, the above principles make it clear that, not only should companies go through a formal process of considering their internal audit and control procedures and evaluating their relationship with their external auditor, but they must be seen to be doing so in a fair and thorough manner. It is, therefore, essential that the Audit Committee is properly constituted with a clear remit and identified authority.

As regards the make up of the Committee, we have followed the Combined Code and recommend a minimum of three independent

---

1 *The Combined Code on Corporate Governance* July 2003, C.3.
2 *The Combined Code on Corporate Governance* July 2003, C.3.2
3 *Audit Committees – Combined Code Guidance* January 2003 1.4 Note that references are to the original version published in January 2003 A slightly modified version of the Smith Guidance, with a different numbering sequence, was appended to the Combined Code published in July 2003

non-executive directors (although two is permissible for smaller companies).[4] The board should satisfy itself that at least one member of the Committee has recent and relevant financial experience. We have made specific recommendations that others may be required to assist the Committee from time to time, according to the particular items being considered and discussed.

Although not a provision in the Code, the Higgs review, states as good practice, in its Non-Code Recommendations, that the company secretary (or their designee) should act as secretary to the Committee.[5] The Smith Report states that the company secretary should attend the Audit Committee. It is the company secretary's responsibility to ensure that the board and its Committees are properly constituted and advised. There also needs to be a clear co-ordination between the main board and the various Committees where the company secretary would normally act as a valued intermediary. In addition, although the responsibility for internal controls clearly remains with the board as a whole, the company secretary would normally have the day-to-day task of reviewing the internal control procedures of the company and responsibility for drafting the governance report.

The frequency with which the Committee needs to meet will vary from company to company and may change from time to time. As a general rule, most Audit Committees would be expected to meet quarterly – the Combined Code provides that the Committee should meet at least three times a year.

The list of duties we have proposed are those which we believe all Audit Committees should consider. Some companies may wish to add to this list and some smaller companies may need to modify it in other ways. The Combined Code includes a provision for a report on

[4] A smaller company is defined as one which is below the FTSE 350 throughout the year immediately before the reporting year.
[5] *Review of the role and effectiveness of non-executive directors,* January 2003 para 11.30

the Audit Committee to be included in the company's annual report.[6] Such report will need to disclose the following:

- Role and main responsibilities of the Audit Committee;
- Composition of committee, including relevant qualifications and experience; the appointment process; and any fees paid in respect of membership;
- Number of meetings and attendance levels;
- A description of the main activities of the year to:
    - Monitor the integrity of the financial statements;
    - Review the integrity of the internal financial control and risk management systems;
    - Review the independence of the external auditors, and the provision of non-audit services;
    - Describe the oversight of the external audit process, and how its effectiveness was assessed;
    - Explain the recommendation to the board on the appointment of auditors.

The Chairman of the Committee should attend the AGM prepared to respond to any questions that may be raised by shareholders on matters within the Committee's area of responsibility.[7] The Combined Code also requires that the terms of reference of the Audit Committee, explaining its role and the authority delegated to it by the board, be made available on request and placed on the company's website.[8]

There is clearly a need for there to be a guiding document for the effective operation of the Audit Committee. This has led the ICSA to produce this Guidance Note proposing model terms of reference for an Audit Committee. The document draws on the experience of senior Company Secretaries and best practice as carried out in some of the country's leading companies.

---

[6] *The Combined Code on Corporate Governance* – July 2003 C.3.3 and *Audit Committees – Combined Code Guidance* 6.1, 6.2

[7] *The Combined Code on Corporate Governance* – July 2003 D.2.3 and *Audit Committees – Combined Code Guidance* 6.3

[8] *The Combined Code on Corporate Governance* – July 2003 C.3.3

Companies which have a US listing may need to amend these terms in light of the requirements of the recently introduced rules following the Sarbanes Oxley Act.

The Combined Code also requires that the terms of reference of the Audit Committee, explaining its role and the authority delegated to it by the board, be made available on request and placed on the company's website.[9]

While this Guidance Note is aimed primarily at the corporate sector, the doctrine of good governance, including the introduction of Audit Committees, is increasingly being recognised and adopted by other organisations particularly in the public and not for profit sectors. The principles underlying the content of this Guidance Note are applicable regardless of the size or type of organisation and we trust that it will be useful across all sectors.

Reference to "the Committee" shall mean the Audit Committee. Reference to "the board" shall mean the board of directors. The square brackets contain recommendations which are in line with best practice but which may need to be changed to suit the circumstances of the particular organisation.

---

1. Membership

1.1 Members of the Committee shall be appointed by the board, on the recommendation of the Nomination Committee in consultation with the Chairman of the Audit Committee. The Committee shall be made up of at least [3] members.

1.2 All members of the Committee shall be independent non-executive directors[10] at least one of whom shall have recent

[9] *The Combined Code on Corporate Governance* A.4.1
[10] An independent non-executive director is defined in Combined Code provision A.3.1

and relevant financial experience. The Chairman of the board shall not be a member of the Committee.[11]

1.3 Only members of the Committee have the right to attend Committee meetings. However, other individuals such as the Chairman of the board, Chief Executive, Finance Director, other directors, the heads of risk, compliance and internal audit and representatives from the finance function may be invited to attend all or part of any meeting as and when appropriate.

1.4 The external auditors will be invited to attend meetings of the Committee on a regular basis.

1.5 Appointments to the Committee shall be for a period of up to three years, which may be extended for two further three year periods, provided the director remains independent.

1.6 The board shall appoint the Committee Chairman who shall be an independent non-executive director. In the absence of the Committee Chairman and/or an appointed deputy, the remaining members present shall elect one of themselves to chair the meeting.

2. Secretary

2.1 The company secretary or their nominee shall act as the secretary of the Committee.

3. Quorum

3.1 The quorum necessary for the transaction of business shall be [2] members. A duly convened meeting of the Committee at which a quorum is present shall be competent to exercise all or any of the authorities, powers and discretions vested in or exercisable by the Committee.

[11] Except on appointment, the Chairman of the company is not considered to meet the test of independence. Combined Code provision A.3.1

4. Frequency of Meetings

4.1 The Committee shall meet [at least three times a year at appropriate times in the reporting and audit cycle] [quarterly on the first Wednesday in each of January, April, July and October] and otherwise as required.[12]

5. Notice of Meetings

5.1 Meetings of the Committee shall be summoned by the secretary of the Committee at the request of any of its members or at the request of external or internal auditors if they consider it necessary.

5.2 Unless otherwise agreed, notice of each meeting confirming the venue, time and date together with an agenda of items to be discussed, shall be forwarded to each member of the Committee, any other person required to attend and all other non-executive directors, no later than [5] working days before the date of the meeting. Supporting papers shall be sent to Committee members and to other attendees as appropriate, at the same time.

6. Minutes of Meetings

6.1 The secretary shall minute the proceedings and resolutions of all meetings of the Committee, including recording the names of those present and in attendance.

6.2 The secretary shall ascertain, at the beginning of each meeting, the existence of any conflicts of interest and minute them accordingly.

6.3 Minutes of Committee meetings shall be circulated promptly to all members of the Committee and, once agreed, to all members of the board.

---

[12] The frequency and timing of meetings will differ according to the needs of the company. Meetings should be organised so that attendance is maximised (for example by timetabling them to coincide with board meetings).

7. **Annual General Meeting**

7.1 The Chairman of the Committee shall attend the Annual General Meeting prepared to respond to any shareholder questions on the Committee's activities.

8. **Duties**

The Committee should carry out the duties below for the parent company, major subsidiary undertakings and the group as a whole, as appropriate.

8.1 Financial Reporting

8.1.1 The Committee shall monitor the integrity of the financial statements of the company, including its annual and interim reports, preliminary results' announcements and any other formal announcement relating to its financial performance, reviewing significant financial reporting issues and judgements which they contain. The Committee shall also review summary financial statements, significant financial returns to regulators and any financial information contained in certain other documents, such as announcements of a price sensitive nature.

8.1.2 The Committee shall review and challenge where necessary:

8.1.2.1 the consistency of, and any changes to, accounting policies both on a year on year basis and across the company/group;

8.1.2.2 the methods used to account for significant or unusual transactions where different approaches are possible;

8.1.2.3 whether the company has followed appropriate accounting standards and made appropriate estimates and judgements, taking into account the views of the external auditor;

8.1.2.4 the clarity of disclosure in the company's financial reports and the context in which statements are made; and

8.1.2.5 all material information presented with the financial statements, such as the operating and financial review and the corporate governance statement (insofar as it relates to the audit and risk management);

8.1.3 The Committee shall review the annual financial statements of the pension funds where not reviewed by the board as a whole.

8.2 Internal Controls and Risk Management Systems

The Committee shall:

8.2.1 keep under review the effectiveness of the company's internal controls and risk management systems; and

8.2.2 review and approve the statements to be included in the annual report concerning internal controls and risk management.[13]

8.3 Whistleblowing

The Committee shall review the company's arrangements for its employees to raise concerns, in confidence, about possible wrongdoing in financial reporting or other matters. The Committee shall ensure that these arrangements allow proportionate and independent investigation of such matters and appropriate follow up action.

[13] Unless this is done by the board as a whole.

8.4 Internal Audit

The Committee shall:

8.4.1 monitor and review the effectiveness of the company's internal audit function in the context of the company's overall risk management system;[14]

8.4.2 approve the appointment and removal of the head of the internal audit function;

8.4.3 consider and approve the remit of the internal audit function and ensure it has adequate resources and appropriate access to information to enable it to perform its function effectively and in accordance with the relevant professional standards. The Committee shall also ensure the function has adequate standing and is free from management or other restrictions;

8.4.4 review and assess the annual internal audit plan;

8.4.5 review promptly all reports on the company from the internal auditors;

8.4.6 review and monitor management's responsiveness to the findings and recommendations of the internal auditor; and

8.4.7 meet the head of internal audit at least once a year, without management being present, to discuss their remit and any issues arising from the internal audits carried out. In addition, the head of internal audit shall be given the right of direct access to the Chairman of the board and to the Committee.

[14] If the company does not have an internal audit function, the Committee should consider annually whether there should be one and make recommendation to the board accordingly. The absence of such a function should be explained in the annual report.

8.5 External Audit

The Committee shall:

8.5.1 consider and make recommendations to the board, to be put to shareholders for approval at the AGM, in relation to the appointment, re-appointment and removal of the company's external auditor. The Committee shall oversee the selection process for new auditors and if an auditor resigns the Committee shall investigate the issues leading to this and decide whether any action is required;

8.5.2 oversee the relationship with the external auditor including (but not limited to):

8.5.2.1 approval of their remuneration, whether fees for audit or non-audit services and that the level of fees is appropriate to enable an adequate audit to be conducted;

8.5.2.2 approval of their terms of engagement, including any engagement letter issued at the start of each audit and the scope of the audit;

8.5.2.3 assessing annually their independence and objectivity taking into account relevant [UK] professional and regulatory requirements and the relationship with the auditor as a whole, including the provision of any non-audit services;

8.5.2.4 satisfying itself that there are no relationships (such as family, employment, investment, financial or business) between the auditor and the company (other than in the ordinary course of business);

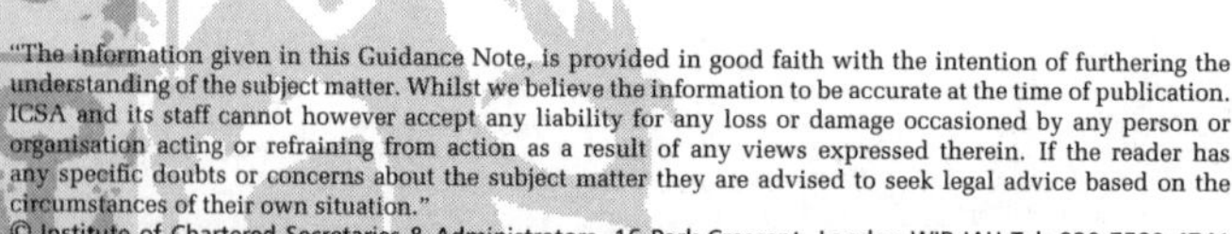

8.5.2.5 agreeing with the board a policy on the employment of former employees of the company's auditor, then monitoring the implementation of this policy;

8.5.2.6 monitoring the auditor's compliance with relevant ethical and professional guidance on the rotation of audit partners, the level of fees paid by the company compared to the overall fee income of the firm, office and partner and other related requirements; and

8.5.2.7 assessing annually their qualifications, expertise and resources and the effectiveness of the audit process which shall include a report from the external auditor on their own internal quality procedures;

8.5.3 meet regularly with the external auditor, including once at the planning stage before the audit and once after the audit at the reporting stage. The Committee shall meet the external auditor at least once a year, without management being present, to discuss their remit and any issues arising from the audit;

8.5.4 review and approve the annual audit plan and ensure that it is consistent with the scope of the audit engagement;

8.5.5 review the findings of the audit with the external auditor. This shall include but not be limited to, the following;

8.5.5.1 a discussion of any major issues which arose during the audit,

8.5.5.2 any accounting and audit judgements, and

8.5.5.3 levels of errors identified during the audit.

The Committee shall also review the effectiveness of the audit.

8.5.6 review any representation letter(s) requested by the external auditor before they are signed by management;

8.5.7 review the management letter and management's response to the auditor's findings and recommendations; and

8.5.8 develop and implement a policy on the supply of non-audit services by the external auditor, taking into account any relevant ethical guidance on the matter.

8.6 Reporting Responsibilities

8.6.1 The Committee Chairman shall report formally to the board on its proceedings after each meeting on all matters within its duties and responsibilities.

8.6.2 The Committee shall make whatever recommendations to the board it deems appropriate on any area within its remit where action or improvement is needed.

8.6.3 The Committee shall compile a report to shareholders on its activities to be included in the company's annual report.

8.7 Other Matters

The Committee shall:

8.7.1 have access to sufficient resources in order to carry out its duties, including access to the company secretariat for assistance as required;

8.7.2 be provided with appropriate and timely training, both in the form of an induction programme for new members and on an ongoing basis for all members;

8.7.3 give due consideration to laws and regulations, the provisions of the Combined Code and the requirements of the UK Listing Authority's Listing Rules as appropriate;

8.7.4 be responsible for co-ordination of the internal and external auditors;

8.7.5 oversee any investigation of activities which are within its terms of reference and act as a court of the last resort; and

8.7.6 at least once a year, review its own performance, constitution and terms of reference to ensure it is operating at maximum effectiveness and recommend any changes it considers necessary to the board for approval.

9. Authority

The Committee is authorised:

9.1 to seek any information it requires from any employee of the company in order to perform its duties;

9.2 to obtain, at the company's expense, outside legal or other professional advice on any matter within its terms of reference; and

9.3 to call any employee to be questioned at a meeting of the Committee as and when required.

October 2003

CG Role of the Company Secretary

ICSA Guidance Notes

Reference Number
021001

ICSA

ICSA Guidance Note

Specimen job description for the Corporate Governance role of the Company Secretary

- Ensuring the smooth running of the board's and board committees' activities by helping the chairman to set agendas, preparing papers and presenting papers to the board and board committees, advising on board procedures and ensuring the board follows them.
- Keeping under close review all legislative, regulatory and corporate governance developments that might affect the Company's operations, and ensuring the board is fully briefed on these and that it has regard to them when taking decisions.
- Ensuring that the concept of stakeholders (particularly employees - see section 309 Companies Act 1985) is in the board's mind when important business decisions are being taken. Keeping in touch with the debate on Corporate Social Responsibility and stakeholders, and monitoring all developments in this area and advising the board in relation to its policy and practices with regard to Corporate Social Responsibility and its reporting on that matter.
- To act as a confidential sounding board to the chairman, non-executive Directors and executive Directors on points that may concern them, and to take a lead role in managing difficult inter-personal issues on the board e.g. the exit of the Directors from the business.
- To act as a primary point of contact and source of advice and guidance for, particularly, non executive Directors

as regards the Company and its activities in order to support the decision making process.

- To act as an additional enquiring voice in relation to board decisions which particularly affect the Company, drawing on his experience and knowledge of the practical aspects of management including law, tax and business finance. To act as the "Conscience of the Company."
- To ensure, where applicable, that the standards and/or disclosures required by the Combined Code annexed to the UK Listing Rules are observed and, where required, reflected in the Annual Report of the Directors – the Secretary usually takes the lead role in drafting the Annual Report, including the Remuneration disclosures and agreeing these with the board and board committee.
- Compliance with the continuing obligations of the Listing Rules e.g. ensuring publications and dissemination of Report and Accounts and interim reports within the periods laid down in the Listing Rules; dissemination of Regulatory News Announcements such as Trading Statements to the market; ensuring that proper notification is made of Directors' dealings and the acquisition of interests in the Company's incentive arrangements.
- Managing relations with investors, particularly institutional investors, with regard to corporate governance issues and the board's practices in relation to corporate governance.
- To induct new Directors into the business and their roles and responsibilities.
- As regards offences under the Financial Services and Markets Act (eg s395), ensuring that the board is fully

Reference Number
021001

ICSA

aware of its responsibility to ensure that it does not mislead the market by putting out or allowing the release of misleading information about its financial performance or trading condition, or by omitting to state information which it should state, or by engaging in a course of conduct which could amount to misleading the market.

- Ensuring compliance with all statutory filings, e.g. forms 288, 88(2), Annual Returns, filing of resolutions adopted at Annual General Meetings/new Articles of Association and any other filings required to be made with Companies House.
- Making arrangements for and managing the whole process of the Annual General Meeting and establishing, with the board's agreement, the items to be considered at the AGM, including resolutions dealing with governance type matters, eg the vote on the Remuneration Report and votes on special incentive schemes involving directors. Information about proxy votes etc.

The above comprises a simple list of the main 'Corporate Governance' activities carried out by the Company Secretary. There are many other matters (e.g. risk management, trading standards etc) for which the Company Secretary will often be responsible and the extent of his other duties will depend on the particular company. Further details of these 'other duties' can be found in the results of an ICSA survey on the Responsibilities and Salaries of Company Secretaries 2000/2001.

Index